Insights

Apartheid: power and historical falsification

Marianne Cornevin

082710

The designations employed and the presentation of material throughout this publication do not imply the expression of any opinion whatsoever on the part of Unesco concerning the legal status of any country, territory, city or area or of its authorities, or concerning the delimitation of its frontiers or boundaries.

Published in 1980 by the United Nations Educational, Scientific and Cultural Organization 7 Place de Fontenoy, 75700 Paris Printed by Imprimerie des Presses Universitaires de France, Vendôme

ISBN 92–3–101769–1
French edition: 92–3–201769–5

Preface

Apartheid: Power and Historical Falsification constitutes part of Unesco's programme of studies undertaken for the International Year against Apartheid, declared by the United Nations on 21 March 1978.

The racist nature of the policies and practices of the Government of South Africa in the fields of education, science, culture and information has been examined in several Unesco studies published under the Organization's programme on southern Africa.

Dr Cornevin's study exposes the false historical premises on which the ideology of apartheid is based and the myths that have been created to justify such an ideology.

The centrepiece of the South African Government's current domestic policy is the creation of 'homelands' whereby 72 per cent of the population is to be settled in ten black 'independent states', each made up of several parcels of largely undeveloped land with scant resources. Together, they would comprise 13 per cent of the land area of South Africa. The whites—16.5 per cent of the population—would retain 87 per cent of the total land area divided in such a way as to include almost all of the country's considerable resources of mineral and agricultural wealth.

South Africa would then become a 'white' state with ten black satellites whose peoples would be deprived of South African nationality and which would subsist largely on direct grants from the South African Treasury.

The 'homelands' policy is justified by one of the most persistent myths—that the first Dutch settlers in South Africa came to an uninhabited land and that the blacks were later immigrants. A subsequent variation of this myth was that both peoples arrived in South Africa at the same time. In either case the blacks are considered to have no prescriptive right to the country nor to the wealth supposedly created by white knowledge and industry alone.

Dr Cornevin presents counter-arguments based on incontrovertible archaeological and anthropological evidence. Equally important, she demonstrates that South African history has been made by blacks as well as whites and that it long antedates white settlement.

Unesco hopes that this publication, while filling an important gap in the literature on apartheid, will be of use to all those who seek information on South Africa.

The author, however, is responsible for the choice and the presentation of the facts contained in this book and for the opinions expressed therein, which are not necessarily those of Unesco and do not commit the Organization.

Contents

Introduction

South Africa is the only country in the world in which racialism is written into the constitution and the only country in which skin colour irrevocably determines the place of a category of nationals in the social hierarchy. Over four-fifths of the national community in South Africa are the victims of apartheid, which for them amounts to the negation of human rights.

As a result the Pretoria government has become the target of virtually the whole international community. It defends itself by an active propaganda campaign aimed at 'justifying' the exorbitant rights of the white minority (16 per cent of the total population in 1979) which alone is entitled to vote for the Parliament of the Republic, 'owns' over 87 per cent of the total area of the country, and receives 70 per cent of the national income.

This campaign to justify apartheid, which is carried on in a wide variety of countries, often by non-South African advocates of a 'white South Africa', continually uses historical arguments. Even in publications dealing exclusively with contemporary social and cultural subjects it is unusual not to come across a historical chapter (or paragraph) that refers to the date (1652) when the 'white African tribe' of Afrikaners established itself at the southern tip of the black continent, and relates it to the time when 'the Bantu from the Great Lakes region' crossed the Limpopo (the northern border of the Republic).

Why are the supporters of apartheid so obsessed with history?

This first question is indisputable, since contemporary political theorists unanimously stress the importance of the historical foundation of a given country to explain its current social structures.

South African society is such that neither blacks nor whites can be considered in isolation. It therefore seemed essential before studying 'Apartheid and the History of South African Blacks' (Part Three) to examine 'Apartheid and the History of South African Whites' (Part Two), so as to clarify the origins of the apartheid ideology and, in particular, the historical religious amalgam that is one of the main components of the Afrikaner identity.

Part One serves as an introduction to the other two parts by giving a definition of the so-called 'territorial or grand' apartheid (first chapter), whose consequences today do not seem to be fully understood. It then studies in detail some 'ideological bases' (second chapter) and concludes with a chapter on 'Apartheid and the Afrikaans Churches'.

In the specific case of South Africa, knowledge of the history of white settlement is obviously essential for an understanding of the development of the racial ideology now prevalent among the white population of South Africa.

Part Two (fourth chapter) gives a detailed account of the emergence of essential features of Afrikaner (60 per cent of the white population) ideology during the 'Dutch period' (1652–1795) and emphasizes the cultural isolation of the two Boer Republics in the nineteenth century. For 250 years the Bible was the sole cultural diet of the vast majority of those who did not live in the immediate neighbourhood of the Cape.

The English-speaking South Africans (37 per cent of the white population) arrived only in the nineteenth century. Their Victorian ideology was characterized by the odd combination of a burning passion for the abolition of slavery and a profound contempt for non-British civilizations in general and coloured peoples in particular. This ideology inspired the many racist laws on job segregation passed between 1911 and 1926, just as it had inspired the Masters and Servants Acts of 1856, which until 1972 governed relations between masters (white) and servants (non-whites).

Now that modern research has yielded new data on the pre-European history of South African blacks, what credence can be given to the historical arguments put forward to justify the inordinate privileges of the white minority?

It is mainly to answer this second question that this study has been undertaken. The reading of even the most recent books devoted partly or entirely to the history of South Africa makes it abundantly clear that these new data are unknown to many self-styled specialists. How much more so then to the general public, which at this time in history has the right to be informed?

For example, twenty years after it was proved that blacks preceded whites in the areas north of the Orange River Valley (i.e. in the provinces of the Orange Free State, Natal and the Transvaal, which account for 80 per cent of South Africa's GNP), the belief in 'simultaneous migrations of whites and blacks' is still often expressed. Though no doubt the most famous, this myth is far from being the only one of its kind. Official South African history is full of falsifications designed either to justify the unjust distribution of land or to denigrate and disparage blacks as compared with whites.

The major myths are set out in Part Three—by far the most important—of this study. After the examination of the linguistic and sociopolitical identity of nine distinct black 'nations' in South Africa (fifth chapter), ten myths about the history of South African blacks from the third century A.D. to 1936 are presented and then refuted (Chapters six to fourteen). A final chapter covers contemporary history to the end of 1978 and examines the conduct of the present government,[1] which would like to preserve South African society in its present form by forgetting that history is made not only by whites but also by blacks.

The many quotations in this paper have been selected so as to exclude all foreign comment. They all come from South African sources and mainly from recent official documents. We have not used the quotations from the 1950s which are continually reproduced in various works on apartheid, but have first and foremost made systematic use of a work widely distributed by the South African embassies and stating what Pretoria would like the rest of the world to know about South Africa, namely the *Official Yearbook of the Republic of South Africa*.[2] This bulky volume, which in its 1977 edition runs to over 1,000 pages, was written and distributed, like the previous three editions, by the Department of Information (which in May 1978 was abolished to become the Bureau for National and International Communication, and was later, in February 1979, renamed the Information Service of South Africa).

Secondly, we have quoted from four school textbooks for Standards 6, 7 and 8 published in English in 1974 and 1975 by Nasou Ltd, a subsidiary of the powerful Cape Town-based Afrikaans publishing group Nasionale Pers.

We have also borrowed extensively from two well-known Afrikaner authors, A. J. van Jaarsveld and W. J. de Klerk, who have both produced very fine studies of Afrikaner psychology as seen from the inside, which is such an important factor in the present deadlock.

1. Awareness of the essential need to bring about economic integration of the blacks prompted F. W. Botha, who has been Prime Minister since 28 September 1978, to announce in September 1979 a greater degree of flexibility in segregation at work and the abandonment of a number of discriminatory measures deemed 'unnecessary'. There is no question, however, of giving up 'multinational development' (the official designation of 'grand apartheid' proper, as opposed to 'petty apartheid'), renamed 'vertical differentiation' by Botha.
2. All the quoted passages appear word for word in *South Africa 1978*.

We have deliberately not quoted from English-speaking South African authors. English-speaking South Africans are admittedly largely responsible for the tragedy in the everyday lives of South African blacks, and are still today the main recipients of the national wealth; over three-quarters of the country's company chairmen are of British origin. But since 1948 they have played a secondary role in politics, and are far less involved in the official history taught in the schools, which is essentially the history of the Afrikaners. The racist myths of the English-speaking population are therefore considered separately in the third chapter, which is devoted to the ideological bases of apartheid.

We hope, in thus using the most recent works (mostly published in the United Kingdom) to refute the falsifications in the official history of South Africa, that we may have made some small contribution to the much-needed rehabilitation of the history of South African blacks—a rehabilitation passionately called for by Steve Biko, who in 1972 wrote in *Essays in Black Theology* (banned in South Africa since its publication): 'Not only is there no objectivity in the history taught us but there is frequently an appalling misrepresentation of facts that sicken even the uninformed student. If we as blacks want to aid each other in our coming into consciousness, we have to rewrite our history. . . .'

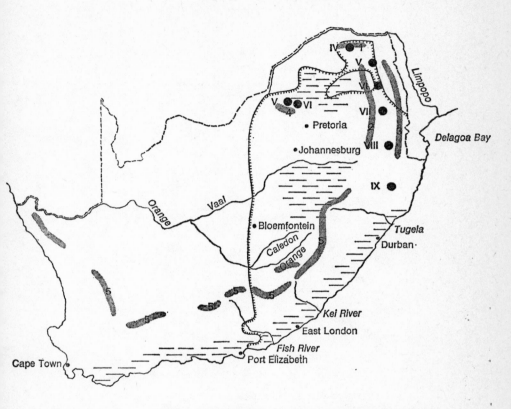

Pretoria   Names of towns or cities to serve as reference points

⟋⟍   Direction of mountain ranges
1   Zoutpansberg
2   Transvaal Drakensberg
3   Lebombo Mts
4   Magaliesberg
5   Various segments of the Great Escarpment

●   Early Iron Age sites dated by carbon-14
                    (centuries in Roman numerals)

⋯⋯⋯   600 mm isohyet

— · —   Scattered Khoisan settlements

FIG. 1. Settlements in South Africa at the end
of the first millennium A.D.

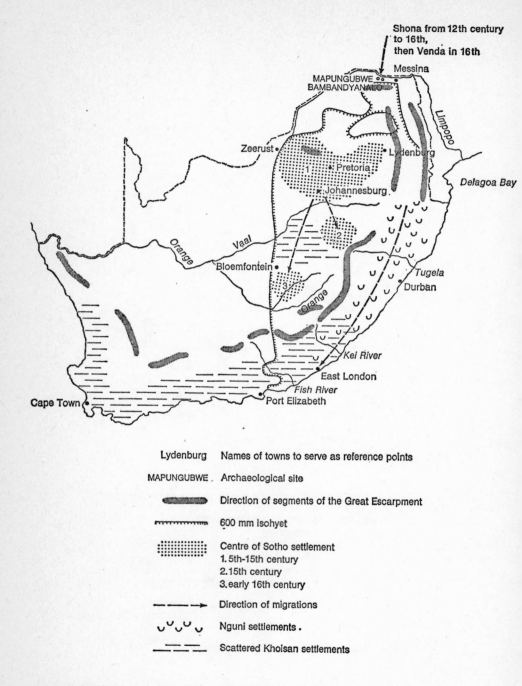

FIG. 2. Settlements in South Africa at the beginning
of the seventeenth century

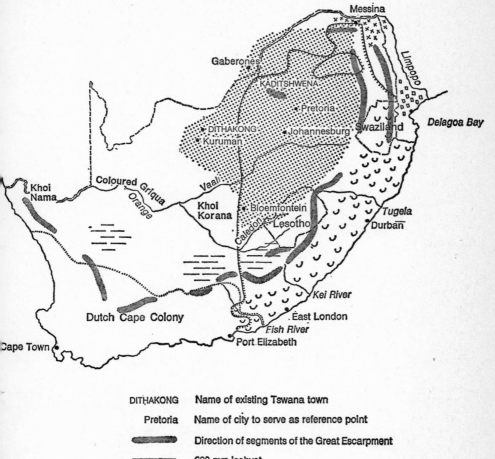

DITHAKONG	Name of existing Tswana town
Pretoria	Name of city to serve as reference point
⬤	Direction of segments of the Great Escarpment
▬▬▬	600 mm isohyet
⠿⠿⠿	Sotho settlements
◡◡◡◡◡	Nguni settlements
◻◻◻◻	Tsonga settlements
˟ˣ˟ˣ	Venda settlements
— — —	Scattered San (Bushmen)

FIG. 3. Settlements in South Africa at the end of the eighteenth century

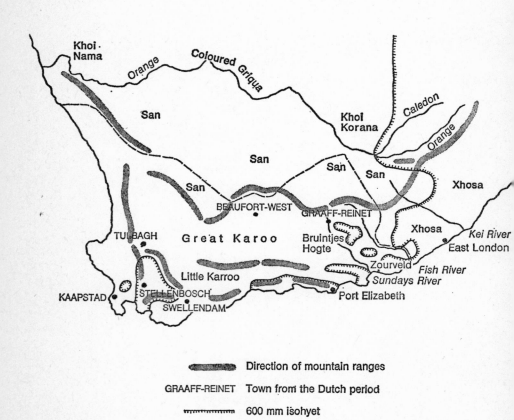

FIG. 4. The Dutch Cape Colony in 1795

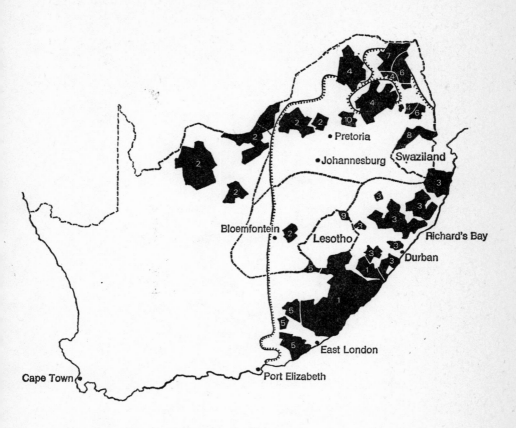

FIG. 5. Position of the homelands in relation
to the 600 mm isohyet

Population distribution in South Africa

In résumé the following table shows that half-way through the century one South African in five was white, and in 1975 one in six. By the end of the century the proportion will be just over one in eight. The figures presented below are in thousands and in percentages of the total population.

TABLE 1. Proportions and trends

Year	1904	1951	1970	1975	2000
Blacks	3 490	8 560	15 058	17 800	37 300
Percentage	67.5	67.6	70.2	71.1	74.2
Whites	1 117	2 642	3 751	4 200	6 900
Percentage	21.6	20.9	17.5	16.5	13.7
Coloured	445	1 103	2 018	2 300	4 900
Percentage	8.6	8.7	9.4	9.5	9.7
Indians	122	367	620	700	1 215
Percentage	2.4	2.9	2.9	2.9	2.4

Census figures for 1904, 1951 and 1970.
Estimate for 1975.
Official forecast for 2000 (by Professor Sadie).

Glossary

The frequent changes of meaning of certain keywords in the South African political vocabulary necessitate a short glossary giving the different names successively or simultaneously used for the same thing.

Africans is used in English-language publications to denote the black majority (71 per cent in 1978) of the South African population. But since the Afrikaans for it is *Afrikaner*, it is not used in official English-language publications, in which the term *black* in 1977 replaced the term *Bantu*, which itself in 1955 superseded the term *native*.

Afrikaners has since the First World War denoted the Afrikaans-speaking descendants (60 per cent of the present white population) of the Dutch, German and French settlers who arrived from 1652 onwards. They were previously called *Boers* (farmers, peasants), *Burghers* or, in the nineteenth century, *Afrikaanders*.

Apartheid means 'separation' or 'setting apart' in Afrikaans. It has been superseded by 'separate development', 'multinational development' or 'pluralist democracy'.

Bantu is a linguistic term collectively defining about a hundred closely related African languages spoken south of the equator. It is derived from the root *ntu*, 'individual', which is common to all these languages. *Umntu* means a person; *Bantu* means several persons. The term *Bantus*, used for South African blacks between 1955 and 1977, is thus doubly wrong, since the word *Bantu* is itself a plural and should only be used in a linguistic sense. For the same reason the use of the plural *s* is inappropriate when referring to Bantu-language ethnic groups.

Blacks: since 1970 the supporters of 'black consciousness' have rejected the use of the 'negative' term *non-white* for the three racial groups, Africans, coloured and Indians, oppressed by the whites, and have adopted the 'positive' collective term *blacks*.

To avoid confusion, however, the term South African *blacks* will in this paper be used only to refer to black Africans, and not to Africans, coloureds and Indians as a whole.

Coloured is the word used to denote the 'racial group' of mixed origin (9.5 per cent of the total population), and is now replaced by *brown* in some documents.

English-speaking South Africans (ESSA) is the name currently given to the 37 per cent of the white population whose mother tongue is English. They were formerly called *British*.

Homeland is the name given since 1972 to the *Bantustans*, which themselves succeeded the *Reserves* officially demarcated in 1913 and 1936.

Indians: 99 per cent of the 'racial group' referred to in official texts as *Asians* (2.9 per cent of the total population) are natives of India and Pakistan who arrived in the province of Natal from 1860 onwards.

Khoisan is a collective term applied to the *Khoi* or *Khoikhoi* (previously called *Hottentots*) and the *San* (previously called *Bushmen*). The very rare descendants of these two peoples live in Namibia (Nama) and Botswana, but are now virtually unrepresented in South Africa.

White has taken the place of 'European' in all official texts since 1971.

Part One:
General information

1 Definition of apartheid

It was only in the immediate post-war period that the word 'apartheid', which in Afrikaans means 'separation' or 'setting apart', came into common use in South African political language as meaning 'separate development of each race in the geographical area assigned to it'.

The word 'apartheid' has often been wrongly used and confused with 'racial segregation' or 'racial discrimination'. In fact the doctrine of separation emerges—at least in its practical expression—as a means of strengthening and perfecting a system of racial discrimination rooted in the mores since the beginning of the eighteenth century with the Afrikaner theory of *baaskap*, and in the law since the nineteenth century with the British pass laws and the Masters and Servants Act.

Between 1910 and 1934, when there was no such thing as South African nationality and when Britain still had theoretical rights over the policies of the Union of South Africa, a complete corpus of legislation was built up determining land-ownership rights, employment and wage conditions, the place and nature of a person's residence, freedom of movement, political rights, the quality of education, etc., on the basis of membership in a racial group.

Long before 1948 police enforcement had already reached perfection. An African could be prosecuted for not carrying his pass, breaking a contract of service, not paying his taxes or his rent, carrying a stick or a knife over a certain length, making or selling beer, taking part in a meeting of over a dozen people, or quite simply for 'idleness'.

'Unequal separation based solely on skin colour' would seem to be the best translation of the word *apartheid*, which has now been officially replaced by the expression 'multi-national development'.

It is well known that the inequality characteristic of apartheid applies from the cradle to the grave and in all aspects of life, whether political, economic or social. Many publications have revealed details of the intolerable administrative and police constraints that burden the daily lives of blacks working in white areas.

But the consequences for blacks of consistent application of the concept of separation have escaped many observers. They are nevertheless dramatic.

The ultimate objective of apartheid is the political division of the present Republic of South Africa into eleven independent states. Ten 'black states', originally called Bantustans and now 'homelands' and each corresponding to an ethnic sub-division, would together contain 72 per cent of the present population and occupy 13 per cent of the area. These ten 'states' would be invited to join an economic federation controlled by the eleventh (white) state, which would comprise a white majority (16.5 per cent of the present population) and two minorities—the coloureds (10 per cent of the present population) and the Indians (2.9 per cent). Both the latter are regarded as second-class citizens and have no vote in the national parliamentary elections.

As long ago as 1950 Dr D. F. Malan (1874–1959), who was Prime Minister from 1948 to 1954, pointed out the impracticable nature of such a division at a time of rapid economic change. 'I made it clear,' he said, 'that territorial apartheid was impracticable in the present circumstances, as the structure of our economy is widely based on the use of African labour.'

The accuracy of this remark has since been all too clearly borne out. In 1976, South African blacks represented 71.6 per cent of the active population, and more than half of them were living in white areas. The number of Africans in relation to the total population varies from province to province. In the Orange Free State four out of five people are Africans; in the Transvaal two out of three; in Natal, just over one in two; and in the Cape Province, where the coloureds are in the majority, one in three. In the 1970 census Pretoria alone of all the large South African cities had a (narrow) white majority.

It is obvious that the economy of white South Africa could not function without the blacks. Moreover, less than half the nationals of the homelands manage to make a living there, since these areas are too small, too fragmented and too

TABLE 2. Land distribution in 1976 (with populations in thousands)

Homeland	De jure nationals	Area (sq. km)	Number of sq. km per 1 000 persons
Republic of South Africa		1 065 000	
Whites	4 300		247
Coloureds	2 400		0
Indians	750		0
Total homelands		155 000	
Blacks	18 600		
Bophuthatswana (Tswana)	2 100	38 000	18
Venda (Venda)	450	6 500	14.4
Lebowa (Northern Sotho) or Bapedi	2 200	22 000	10
Transkei (Xhosa)	4 200	41 000	9.7
Gazankulu (Shangaan-Tsonga)	810	6 800	8.3
KwaZulu (Zulu)	5 000	31 000	6.4
Swazi (Swazi)	590	3 700	6.2
Ciskei (Xhosa)	870	5 300	6
South Ndebele (Southern Ndebele)	240	750	3
Qwaqwa (Southern Sotho or Shweshwe)	1 700	480	0.3

poor in resources. Table 2 shows the number of square kilometres allocated per 1,000 persons in each of the ten black homelands and in the white homeland. The figures have been calculated on the basis of the official population estimates for 1976. Since the coloureds and Indians do not have homelands, they do not appear in the calculation.

The range is thus from 247 sq. km per 1,000 whites in the white homeland to 0.3 sq. km per 1,000 of the southern Sotho Qwaqwa. In view of the fact that approximately one-third of the white homeland is virtual desert, the area per 1,000 persons is reduced to 160 sq. km. This is 530 times more than the area allocated to 1,000 southern Sotho, and 25 times more than that for 1,000 Zulu.

For the 9.5 million blacks living in the white homeland, the political consequences of apartheid appear even more striking than the economic consequences of land distribution for the 8.5 million blacks actually (*de facto*) living in the homelands in 1976.

Following the 'independence' of Transkei on 26 October 1976, Bophutatswana on 6 December 1977 and Venda on 13 September 1979 (which was recognized only by South Africa), about 2 million Xhosa, 1 million Tswana and

TABLE 3. The black population (in millions) in 1976 and 1977: official figures and actual figures before and after the 'independence' of the Transkei (26/10/76) and Bophuthatswana (6/12/77)

	25/10/76	27/10/76	5/12/77	7/12/77
Total black population	18.6	18.6	19.5	19.5
Blacks of South African nationality	18.2	16.3	17	16.1
Foreign blacks	0.4	2.3	2.5	3.4
Total population according to Pretoria	26.1	23.7	24.9	24
Actual total	26.1	26.1	27.4	27.4
Percentage of blacks in the total population				
According to Pretoria	71.1	68.7	68.2	67
Actual	71.1	71.1	71.1	71.1

300,000 Venda living in the white homeland lost their right to a South African passport. They thus became foreigners in what had once been their own country, whose wealth they and their fathers had helped to create.

In the *Bulletin of Statistics* for the last quarter of 1976, the independence of the Transkei is reflected in a decrease in the number of South African blacks corresponding to the *de facto* population of the Transkei, which is given as just over 2 million, and an increase in the number of foreign blacks living in South Africa corresponding to the introduction into the statistics of the 1,760,000 Xhosa now regarded as 'citizens' of the Transkei, even if their family has been living in a white area for three generations.

The number of South African blacks thus officially drops from 18,136,000 in 1975 to 16,279,000 in 1976, whereas unmanipulated statistics record 18,629,000 South African blacks at the end of 1976.

Reflecting the independence of Bophutatswana at the end of 1977, the *Bulletin of Statistics* for the first quarter of 1978 shows a further decrease in the black population to 16,108,000. (See Table 3.)

The final outcome of these successive jugglings would supposedly be as follows: assuming that the ten homelands became independent, this would result in a 'white' State that would exclude all the Africans whose labour contributed enormously to the wealth of the country. Still in hypothetical terms, and taking Professor Sadie's population forecasts for the year 2000 (see Table 1), this white state would contain 6 to 7 million whites, 5 million coloureds and 1.2 million

Indians. Actually, this white state would contain about 20 million blacks needed for the working of its economy, while the homelands would contain 17 million blacks. In the so-called white state, therefore, there would still be four non-whites, including three Africans, to every white, as against five non-whites (including 4.3 Africans) in 1975.

These figures give an idea of the unrealistic nature of territorial apartheid and lead one to question the ideological foundations of a doctrine that seeks to perpetuate an archaic form of society.

2 The ideological bases of apartheid

The absolute superiority of the white race and the need to safeguard its political and economic supremacy are the twin cornerstones of the ideology of apartheid. The superiority of whites to blacks is a conviction deeply rooted in the subconscious of all white South Africans.

Although it has long been publicly stated that 'the most superior black is by definition inferior to the lowest White', and although to this day the unwritten rule that a white cannot be placed under the orders of a black is everywhere applied, the official version of this dogma has become somewhat less virulent. In *South Africa 1977*, for example, we read: 'The white nation is culturally, economically and politically the most advanced group in the country. . . . By contrast, the various black nations may be generally described as developing peoples.'[1]

This feeling of superiority on the part of white South Africans is not confined to their own country, as may be seen from various passages in *South Africa 1977*. For example:

Economically, socially and educationally the white South African nation is today the best developed and politically the most stable community in Africa. . . . In terms of per capita income and mean educational attainment this group is among the half dozen leading nations of the world.[2]

Reverting to South Africa, it should be noted that the idea of 'superiority' is readily replaced in the official literature by that of 'difference'. Thus in the chapter in *South Africa 1977* devoted to multinational development we read:

The fundamental objective of the program of multinational development . . . is self-determination for *all* its peoples . . . The

1. *South Africa 1977*, p. 209.
2. Ibid., p. 76.

Government's approach is not based on any notion of superiority or inferiority, but on the fact that people differ in their historical origins, group associations, loyalties, cultures, and ways of living.[1]

But this disclaimer of the idea of the superiority of the white race is less than convincing in view of the number of paragraphs in the same chapter explaining the white nation's mission of trusteeship. We read on the first page of the chapter: 'During the nineteenth century, several autonomous black peoples came under the political sphere of influence of whites who felt themselves obliged to implement a policy of responsible trusteeship towards these black peoples.' And twenty lines further on: 'A historical heritage has placed the white nation of the Republic of South Africa (RSA) in a position of trusteeship over several developing black peoples.'[2]

The backwardness of the black peoples, the justification for white trusteeship, is repeatedly stressed; for example: 'White South Africa is committed to develop the distinctive peoples, many of whom are only at the beginning of the long road towards self-government and economic and technological self-sufficiency.'[3]

Thus the racist ideology of apartheid is cleverly masked by two loftier topics: (a) the diversity of peoples, and (b) the white race's mission to provide assistance.

These two ways of camouflaging the racism that underlies the apartheid system are widely accepted, not only by South African whites but also, it must be said, by a majority of whites the world over.

In South Africa and elsewhere the supporters of apartheid directly link the theme of the 'diversity of peoples' with that of the 'congenital inferiority of the black race', the 'inferiority' being 'proven' on supposedly scientific grounds in hundreds of publications. Arguments based on cranial measurements and brain structure have less impact now than at the end of the nineteenth century. But physical anthropology has not been completely abandoned. In 1969, for example, a scientific publication maintained that the 'inability of the Negro African in mathematics is due to the underdevelopment of his frontal lobes'.[4]

Just as genetics and comparative psychology have been used to demonstrate the 'biological superiority of the Aryan race' (with consequences that are all too well known), they are invoked to explain the hereditary nature of the 'lack of ability of the black race', which accounts for its 'cultural backwardness'.

1. Ibid., p. 210.
2. Ibid., p. 203.
3. Ibid., p. 210.
4. *The Mankind Quarterly*, Vol. 2, 1969, p. 62.

The fact that this reasoning was an excuse for the massacre of millions of Jews has unfortunately failed to convince some people of the noxious nature of such theories when applied to other peoples. Throughout the Western world there are still people ready to welcome pseudo-scientific arguments as confirmation of their ethnocentric prejudices.

In South Africa this pseudo-scientific argument has a powerful impact on all levels of the white population. Afrikaans-speaking South Africans (60 per cent of white South Africans) are, however, even more receptive to theological arguments about the diversity of peoples and the white race's mission of assistance to primitive peoples. Indeed, 87 per cent of them belong to one of the three Dutch Reformed Churches that have strenuously defended apartheid on the authority of Holy Scripture (see next chapter).

Among the quotations from the Old Testament most often invoked to justify God's ordination of the diversity of peoples and their territorial separation are the episode of the Tower of Babel (Genesis 11: 8): 'So the Lord scattered them abroad from thence upon the face of all the earth'; and the passage from the Canticle of Moses: 'When the Most High divided to the nations their inheritance, when he separated the sons of Adam, he set the bounds of the people according to the number of the children of Israel' (Deuteronomy 32: 8).[1] In the New Testament, the Acts of the Apostles uses more or less the same language: 'And hath made of one blood all nations of men for to dwell on all the face of the earth, and hath determined the times before appointed, and the bounds of their habitation' (Acts 17: 26).

Afrikaner theologians have also made great use of the theme of the curse of Ham, younger son of Noah, father of Canaan and supposedly the ancestor of the black race. It is useful in the context of this study to re-read the verses on which this falsification is based, recalling that it has been invoked by earlier theologians to 'justify' the slavery of black Africans.

Genesis 9: 20–24 recounts how Noah, the ancestor of all the nations that peopled the earth after the Flood, became drunk and was caught naked by his son Ham, who told his brothers Shem and Japheth. 'And Noah awoke from his wine, and knew what his younger son had done unto him. And he said, Cursed be Canaan; a servant of servants shall he be unto his brethren' (Genesis 9: 24–25).

Genesis 10: 6–20 lists the descendants of Ham and specifies the areas where their posterity settled. At no time

1. All the biblical quotations in this book are from the Authorized (King James) Version.

did any of them settle anywhere on the African continent. We read, for example, in verses 19 and 20: 'And the border of the Canaanites was from Sidon, as thou comest to Gerar, unto Gaza; as thou goest, unto Sodom, and Gomorrah, and Admah, and Zeboim, even unto Lasha.'

Therefore in making Ham (the father of Canaan the accursed) the ancestor of African blacks, the exegetists are obviously guilty of a gross falsification, because of the exclusive Eurocentrism that held sway through the nineteenth century and has by no means completely disappeared today.

Nowadays people no longer look to the curse of Ham to explain the so-called 'congenital inferiority' of black South Africans. Yet the idea that the Afrikaners are God's chosen people with a special vocation is still commonly voiced. A case in point is P. J. Cilliers, editor-in-chief of the Afrikaans daily *Die Burger*, who wrote in 1976: 'Africa's unique white tribe of Afrikaners . . . see themselves as a sort of Israel in Africa, with a sense of God-guided destiny that it would be as perilous to discount as in the case of the original model.'[1]

Three ideas seem closely linked to the idea of a 'chosen people'. The first is that this chosen people is endowed with the 'divine mission' of guiding and civilizing African peoples. The Acts of the Apostles and the Epistles of St Paul furnish many quotations that can be used in this sense. The second is that this 'chosen people' cannot and must not interbreed with other peoples: hence the enactment of sexual prohibitions (the 1927 Immorality Act, amended in 1950 and 1956). The third is that the 'chosen people's' right of ownership over the land is inalienable, because it is the 'promised' land given by God. These consequences of the 'chosen people' ideology will be developed in later chapters.

The need to safeguard the 'white South African nation' is forcefully affirmed in the official literature as being at the root of the conception of the apartheid system. The chapter in *South Africa 1977* on 'History', states:

From 1949 onwards the Malan Government introduced legislation to implement the policy of multinational development of the population groups in South Africa. This was considered the only means by which the continued existence of the white South African nation could be safeguarded and the only guarantee of peace in a multinational country.[2]

. 'The Case for Africa's White Tribe', *South Africa 1977*, p. 899.
. Ibid., p. 55.

Put more simply, apartheid is designed above all to ensure the 'survival' of the whites in the face of the rising tide of blacks.

Electoral propaganda even goes so far as to speak of the 'suicide of the white nation' and a 'return to barbarism' if apartheid is not implemented. The fact that the two ideas of 'survival' and 'implementation of apartheid' are so closely linked in the subconscious of Afrikaners explains the irrational nature of their arguments—and the difficulty foreigners experience in discussing the situation with them.

The fact is that the apartheid system, now known as multinational development, was designed and implemented to preserve both political hegemony and the recruitment (from impoverished native reserves) of cheap black labour. However in the chapter in *South Africa 1977* on 'Multinational development' economic questions are entirely avoided and replaced by a discussion of the national identity of the various peoples of South Africa. Thus:

The first reality of the South African situation is that the Whites will only be able to maintain their national identity as long as they control their own political destiny in that part of South Africa which history has given them as their homeland, namely the RSA.[1]

Three pages later, in paragraphs 19 and 21 of the long discussion about 'the alternative to integration', the following arguments are put forward:

A one-man one-vote system for the whole of South Africa would destroy the white nation's distinctive political organization and way of life. [The white nation] would have to change its customs and abandon its culture and vested political interests in order to accommodate the culture, life-style and political needs of a purely numerically determined majority group.[2]

These two quotations—and indeed the whole twenty-two-page chapter in which the foreign reader finds an explanation and justification for multinational development—lead to the following conclusion: Just as the Afrikaners disguise the theme of absolute white superiority in the more respectable garb of the 'difference between peoples' and the 'whites' mission of trusteeship', so they conceal the preservation of the whites' inordinate economic privileges under the cover of protecting 'white identity', and more specifically 'Afrikaner identity'.

In both cases we have a system of justification constructed *a posteriori* to lend respectability to a questionable basic ideology—which is nowadays questioned by the international community.

1. *South Africa 1977*, p. 21
2. Ibid., p. 214.

3 Apartheid and the Afrikaans churches

Apart from history, which will be considered later, the Afrikaans language and Calvinist Protestantism are the essential components of the Afrikaner identity.

It is the special characteristics of Afrikaner society that make it particularly puzzling to outsiders, especially those who have had a secular upbringing. Three components are absolutely inseparable: Afrikaans is the exclusive vehicle of Afrikaner history and religion; history, traditionally presented as that of a chosen people placed by God at the southern tip of Africa to fulfil a divine mission, is based on the Calvinist faith of the first Dutch, German and French settlers, who arrived in the seventeenth century; and religion, in accordance with the pattern set by Calvin in Geneva, has always been closely linked to politics.

The religious content of the ideology of apartheid, will be discussed in the chapter on history. It is essential to devote space here to the bodies responsible for revealing religious doctrine, namely the three Afrikaans churches, referred to collectively as the Dutch Reformed Churches.

The most important and oldest of the three so-called Dutch Reformed Churches is the Nederduitse Gereformeerde Kerk (NGK). Comprising 72 per cent of Afrikaners (or more than 40 per cent of the white population), the NGK goes back to 1665 and the arrival of the first 'resident' minister responsible for the pastoral care of some 400 Calvinists who had settled at the southern tip of Africa. Until 1805 (the second British occupation of the Cape), all the ministers were Dutchmen trained in Holland. In the first half of the nineteenth century the British Government recruited several Scots ministers (Calvinists), until the NGK, which, by 1843 had

achieved relative independence, set up its own seminary at
Stellenbosch in 1859.

Meanwhile, the Voortrekkers, feeling that the NGK owed
too much allegiance to British authority, had founded two
other Dutch Reformed Churches in the Transvaal: the
Nederduitsch Hervormde Kerk (NHK) in 1853, and the
Gereformeerde Kerk (GK) or Doppers' Church (established
in the Transvaal by the future president, Paul Kruger)
in 1859.

Although the majority of Afrikaners in the Transvaal
and the Orange Free State joined the NGK, these two
churches remained dissident, and have their own Faculties
of Theology at Pretoria (NHK) and Potchefstroom (GK).
They comprise respectively 10 and 5 per cent of Afrikaans-
speaking people (or 6 and 3 per cent of the total white
population).

None of the churches, not even the NGK, in South
Africa is subsidized. All the State does is pay the chaplains
of the various denominations who are responsible for giving
the compulsory religious instruction in the army and the
police force. Despite this financial independence it is impossible to speak of the 'separation of Church and State' as
regards the three Dutch Reformed Churches, least of all
the NGK.

The NGK is the church of the South African Establishment. The great majority of senior political and administrative officials regularly attend Sunday service, and, in
a society in which patronage is decisive, bring in their
wake everyone who needs to demonstrate allegiance to a
superior in order to obtain a place in the power hierarchy.
The many family alliances between NGK ministers and
politicians have influenced certain government decisions and
continue visibly to do so. A well-known example is that of
the two Vorster brothers, Johannes Balthazar, who was
Prime Minister between 1966 and 1978 and then President
of the Republic,[1] and J. D. (or Koot) Vorster, who was both
Moderator of the NGK in the Cape Province between 1970
and 1975 and also Chairman of the National Council against
Communism.

The special relationship between the State and the NGK
is so strong and so specific that in order to understand the
behaviour of the present government in a rapidly changing
world we need to probe its historical origins.

1. J. B. Vorster had to re-
on 4 June 1979 and was
replaced as President of th
Republic by Marais Viljoe

The NGK and the Afrikaner Nationalists before 1948

The first National Party (Nasionale Party), which gave rise to the National Party that has been in power since 1948, was founded in 1914 by General J. B. M. Hertzog (1866–1947), the hero of the Boer War and champion of equality between English and Afrikaans in education and the public services. In its programme the party defined itself as 'Christian Nationalist', seeking to develop a South African 'national' life (the Union of South Africa was then only four years old) in accordance with the major principles of the Christian religion, to attain independence in the future. Its 'native policy' (there was no talk of 'Bantu' in those days) was based partly on domination by the 'European' population, exercising its trusteeship over the 'primitive' peoples in a Christian spirit, and partly on the utter necessity of avoiding racial intermixing.

This programme complemented the missionary policy of the NGK, whose ninth synod in 1857 had decided not to accept any more 'pagan converts' into the white parish communities. Separate mission churches, called 'daughter' churches of the NGK, had been set up in 1881: the Nederduitse Gereformeerde Sendingkerk for the coloureds, the NGK in Afrika (which in 1975 became the Black NG Kerk in Afrika) for the blacks, and the Indian Reformed Church for Indians.

The 'Christian Nationalist' programme of the first National Party was also adopted by the early members of the Broederbond (Band of Brothers), founded in 1918 as an official Afrikaner mutual-help association, which became a secret society in 1924.

The congruence between the aims pursued by the National Party, the NGK and the Broederbond was, however, to remain more or less theoretical until 1934, when the former NGK minister Daniel François Malan joined the Broederbond.

Malan (1874–1959) studied theology at Stellenbosch (near Cape Town) and at Utrecht, and was appointed an NGK minister in 1905. He gave up his ministry in 1915 to become editor of *Die Burger*, the newspaper of Hertzog's National Party, and party leader in Cape Province. In 1924, when Hertzog was appointed Prime Minister, Malan obtained the post of Minister of the Interior. In 1934, having refused to accept the fusion of Hertzog's and Smut's parties, he founded the Herenigde Nasionale Party or Volksparty (the Purified National Party, or People's Party). It was to win the 1948 elections under this name, and in 1951 to be renamed the National Party. The foundation of the Purified National Party coincided with Hitler's coming to power as well as the arrival in South Africa of nearly 4,000 German Jewish refugees (2,500 of whom came in 1936).

According to the Afrikaner genealogist J. A. Heese, the Germanic element in the Afrikaner people (the largest, reaching 34.8 per cent) derives from regular German immigration in all periods, with a perceptible increase in the nineteenth century. This close kinship with European Germans is one of the reasons for the keen sympathy for Germany and the Hitler doctrine shown by many Afrikaners. Another reason, also put forward by Afrikaners of Dutch and French origin, 33.7 and 13.2 per cent respectively, is that any increase in German power represented a reduction in British power, and hence an opportunity for the Afrikaners to re-establish the two pre-1902 Boer Republics.

Because of the presence of some ten thousand Germans in the former German colony of South West Africa (Namibia), the Berlin Government was very well aware of the pro-German sympathies professed by a large number of Afrikaners, in particular by the members of the Herenidge Nasionale Party. In 1934, following contacts with Malan, Count von Durckheim Montmartin was given the task of finding out from the leaders of the Broederbond which side South Africa would join in the event of a world war. After his visit the Broederbond was reorganized into groups and cells on the Nazi model. In 1935 N. J. Diederichs, one of the leaders of the secret society, was sent to Germany at Berlin's expense to study the methods of the Nazi party (Diederichs was to become Minister of Economy and Finance in the Verwoerd and Vorster governments, and later President of the Republic until his death in 1978).

As early as 1936 Germans played a part in the setting up of new fascist organizations protesting the arrival of the Jewish refugees, such as the Greyshirts and the Boerenasie (Boer Nation). In 1938 the Greyshirts officially joined Malan's party.

In the case of the party itself, its associated organizations and the Broederbond secret society, the co-operation of the NGK was gained by a clever adaptation of Hitlerian National Socialism to Afrikaner Christian Nationalism. A good example was the 1938 celebration organized on the initiative of the Broederbond to mark the centenary of the 'heroic year' of the Great Trek; 1838 had witnessed the killing of Piet Retief and his men on 6 February, followed by the defeat of the Zulu king Dingaan at the battle of Blood River on 16 December. During the celebration the local parish communities played a key role in the extraordinary patriotic fervour displayed by the crowds, who dressed in period costumes and travelled in ox-wagons to the hill near Pretoria where the first stone of the Voortrekker Monument was laid on 16 December.

It was this great upsurge of popular feeling that led in October to the foundation in Bloemfontein (the capital of the Orange Free State, the most 'Afrikaner' of the four provinces), of the Ossewa Brandwag (Ox-wagon Guard). Not surprisingly, the first chairman of the Groot Raad (Great Council) was a famous Bloemfontein *predikant*, Dominie C. R. Kotze. But while it proclaimed eminently 'cultural' aims, the Ossewa Brandwag was a fascist-style para-military organization which was to undergo an extraordinary expansion in 1940. It had 300,000 members by 1942.

Following an immense sabotage offensive designed to reduce South Africa's military contribution to the war against Germany, thousands of members of the Ossewa Brandwag were interned. They included J. B. Vorster and C. R. Swart, who in 1961 became the first President of the Republic of South Africa.

The ministers of the three Dutch Reformed Churches belonged to the Federasie van Afrikaanse Kulturvereenigings (FAK) founded in 1929, rather than to the Ossewa Brandwag. In 1939 the FAK organized a conference in Bloemfontein on education. Here it was decided to use all available means to foster in schoolchildren of Afrikaner origin 'a sense of pride in belonging to God's chosen people' and to organize 'separate lower-level education for non-whites'.

Afrikaner ministers also belonged to the Broederbond, although exact figures are not known because of the secret nature of the organization. In 1944 Dominie V. de Vos broke with the NGK on the grounds that it was totally controlled by the Broederbond, whose 3,000-strong membership at that time was said to include more than 1,000 teachers and more than 350 ministers (12 per cent). In 1946, Senator Conroy stated in the South African Parliament that 90 per cent of the ministers of the Afrikaner churches were under the influence of the Broederbond.

Even if these figures are open to question, there can be

no doubt about the thorough politicization of the Dutch Reformed Churches, all three of which sent representatives to the 'Afrikaner Front'. This was the body responsible for drawing up a draft constitution in 1941 for the new Republic of South Africa that was supposed to come into being after the defeat of the Allies, an event expected and hoped for by the so-called 'Malanites'. With representatives of the FAK, the RDB (Reddingsdaadbond, a fund for helping 'poor whites'), the OB (Ossewa Brandwag) and the Herenidge Nasionale Party (Purified National Party), the three ministers delegated to the Front signed in their own names the draft that was to be published in revised form on 22 and 23 January 1942 in the Afrikaans newspapers *Die Transvaler* and *Die Burger*.

The first two articles of the introduction, by Dr Malan himself, bore the stamp of his theological training:

In obedience to God Almighty and His Holy Word, the Afrikaans people acknowledge their national destination, as embodied in their Voortrekker past, for the Christian development of South Africa. . . . The Republic is grounded on a Christian-National foundation and therefore acknowledges, as the standard of the government of the State, in the first place the principles of justice of the Holy Scriptures. . . .[1]

After the turning-point of the Russian victory at Stalingrad, the hopes of Malan's followers for a German victory quickly faded. Other threats were looming, this time on the domestic front. They were to act both as a diversion and as a rallying point for the Afrikaner electorate. The rapid urbanization of the blacks resulting from the wartime economic boom was leading towards a dangerous clash with the white working class over housing and jobs.

In preparation for the 1938 elections, the Nationalist Party Congress had already discussed the 'native policy' to be adopted in the future Afrikaner republic, and had announced the broad lines of such a policy: 'This Congress regards the dominant position of the white race in the spirit of guardianship as of vital importance to the future and welfare of South Africa. It declares therefore that it must be the earnest and determined struggle of that race to preserve its racial purity.'[2] And Dr Malan had proclaimed: 'We want to make sure that South Africa remains a white man's country.'

Despite the triumph of the Smuts government in the 1943 elections, the National Party increased its number of seats from twenty-seven to forty-three.

1. B. Bunting, *The Rise of the South African Reich*, p. 107.
2. Ibid., p. 80.

At the end of the war the great fascist organizations were totally discredited, but the National Party continued to enjoy considerable prestige. Malan then made very adroit use of the research done at Stellenbosch University on a system of 'total racial separation' or apartheid; this system had the approval of two eminent NGK theologians, who contributed biblical quotations 'justifying' such 'divinely ordained' separation to G. Cronje's major book on this subject, published in 1947.[1]

The NGK and the government between 1948 and 1966

It is therefore not surprising that in the 1950s the three Dutch Reformed Churches continually and wholeheartedly supported the doctrine of apartheid.

The backing given to the Afrikaner State by the Afrikaans churches seemed all the more natural since Malan's successors as Prime Minister, J. G. Strijdom (1954–58) and H. F. Verwoerd (1958–66) were likewise members of the Broederbond and cherished the same idea of the State. The countless quotations that bear witness to this are all summed up in Article II of the Constitution of the new South African Republic, which was published in 1960 and came into force on 31 May 1961 on the fifty-first anniversary of the founding of the Union of South Africa: 'The People of the Republic of South Africa acknowledge the sovereignty and help of Almighty God.'

The Cottesloe Conference (December 1960)

Nevertheless the Sharpeville killings of black protestors on 21 March 1960 set off a series of arguments within the Dutch Reformed Churches—and particularly in the NGK—about the incompatibility of apartheid with the teachings of the Gospel.

In December 1960 a conference organized by the World Council of Churches (WCC) at Cottesloe, near Johannesburg, was attended by ten representatives of each of the eight protestant churches in South Africa affiliated to the WCC, including two Afrikaans churches, the NGK and the NHK. The delegates of the NHK were the only ones to oppose the final report. The NGK delegates adopted it, and in so doing demonstrated the acute nature of the crisis of conscience that prevailed within their church. For this report was really

1. G. Cronje, *Regverdige Rasse-apartheid*, Stellenbosch, 1947. Extracts and comments translated in W. de Klerk, *The Puritans in Africa*, p. 215–21.

explosive. Not content with opposing all social segregation within the churches, it went much further: it denounced the absence of any scriptural support for the laws against mixed marriages, deplored the disastrous effects of migrant labour on the family life of blacks, and, above all, acknowledged that blacks settled in white areas were entitled to own land and to take part in government. Moreover, the authors of the report saw no objection to the direct representation of coloureds in Parliament.

These were absolute heresies, which the government could not possibly accept. Its reaction was immediate. In his New Year message to the nation, Prime Minister Verwoerd called the theologians to order in no uncertain terms. The ruling authority of the NGK reacted no less swiftly. On the recommendation of Dominie J. D. Vorster (the brother of J. B. Vorster, then Minister of Justice) the NGK Synod massively rejected the Cottesloe report and decided to break with the World Council of Churches.

A. P. Treurnicht, editor of the weekly *Die Kerkbode*, used its pages to try to convince his readers (all NGK ministers) of the falsehood of the arguments put forward at Cottesloe. In a series of resounding articles, published together in 1965,[1] he explained that 'the only way of obeying divine law is to let each nation express its own identity within the framework of separate development, since each nation is a distinct entity resulting from a specific command by God, who planned its particular inner structure'.

Convinced, or pretending to be so in order to avoid confrontation, virtually all the NGK ministers very quickly reverted to the Neo-Calvinist order preached by Treurnicht.

The Christian Institute (1963–77)

Virtually all, but not quite. The Rev. Beyers Naudé, Moderator (the hierarchical equivalent of a Catholic bishop) of the NGK in the Transvaal, who had been one of his church's representatives at Cottesloe, brought together Christians of different denominations who, like he, had been shocked by the appalling consequences of the application of apartheid for the majority of South Africans who did not belong to the 'chosen race' of whites. In March 1962 they founded the monthly journal *Pro Veritate* with the aim of maintaining a dialogue with the World Council of Churches and the other churches in South Africa. In March 1963 Beyers Naudé gave up his post as Moderator, resigned from the Broederbond, which his father (a minister like himself and an

1. A. P. Treurnicht, *Op die Keper*, 1965. Many extracts translated in W. de Klerk, *The Puritans in Africa*, p. 253–60.

uncompromising defender of Afrikaans culture) had helped to found, and became director of the Christian Institute for Southern Africa, a community of Christians of different 'races' and from different denominations resolved to demonstrate both inside and outside South Africa that apartheid was incompatible with the teachings of the Gospel.

According to the *Sunday Times* of 24 March 1973, more than 40 per cent of the ministers of the three Dutch Reformed Churches were at that time members of the Broederbond or the Ruiterwag, its 'youth' branch founded in 1958. The NGK's reaction was therefore immediate and brutal. Beyers Naudé was at once relieved of his post as a minister and branded a traitor to his people and his church throughout the Afrikaans press, both religious and secular. The 1966 synod decided to take disciplinary action against those NGK ministers who belonged to the Christian Institute. At the same time the National Council against Communism, under the chairmanship of Dominie J. D. Vorster, Moderator of the NGK in Cape Province, accused the Institute of 'undermining the spiritual resistance of the Afrikaner people, working in collaboration with the Catholics, the Protestants' age-old enemies, and holding multiracial meetings strictly forbidden in Holy Scripture'.[1]

The NGK and the government from 1968 to 1978

In 1971 and again in 1973 the premises of the Christian Institute, which was moving towards greater black participation in its work, were subject to massive searches. The Institute had given financial support to the Black Community Programme (BCP) in which Steve Biko was working, and had also appointed to its governing body such blacks as Dr Manas Buthelezi, the world-famous Lutheran theologian and cousin of Chief Gatsha Buthelezi, and Mrs Jane Phakati, chairman of the South African YWCA. These two leaders were to be among the founders of the Black Parents Association (BPA), launched in Soweto after the riots of June 1976. Jane Oshadi Phakati was to be imprisoned, from August to December 1976, and tortured. She managed to leave South Africa clandestinely in May 1977.

On 28 May 1975, after a two-year inquiry by a parliamentary commission, the Christian Institute was declared an 'affected organization', and was thus prevented from raising funds abroad. The effect of the sentence was para-

1. *Die Kerkbode*, February 1966. Quoted in A. M. Goguel and P. Buis, *Chrétiens d'Afrique du Sud face à l'Apartheid*, 1978, p. 64.

lytic, since 91 per cent of its budget came from the Protestant countries of Europe and America.

On 18 September 1976 the Christian Institute, which had managed to survive on South African donations, launched a public appeal in which it:

Called upon the government to give way to a national convention representative of all peoples of South Africa, including those detained or in exile.

Supported the goals of the black political movements (e.g. the African National Congress, the Pan-African Congress, the South African Students' Organization, the Black Peoples Convention and the South African Students' Movement) consonant with biblical values of justice, freedom and human responsibilities.

Reaffirmed its support for all peaceful efforts to bring change, including work stayaways, economic sanctions, and the discouragement of immigration.

Recognized the right of the oppressed to seek freedom for themselves and their oppressors.[1]

In signing such a declaration the Christian Institute was signing its own death warrant. The delayed execution was to take place thirteen months later. On 19 October 1977, five weeks after the death of Steve Biko, the father of Black Consciousness, in prison, the Christian Institute became one of a group of nineteen illegal organizations. Its publications and all its property were seized and its permanent staff 'banned'. Since 1978, no one in South Africa is allowed to quote anything written by the 'former' Christian Institute.

The General Synod of October 1978

The 'civil death' of the Christian Institute left unresolved two problems which its work had exacerbated if not raised. They concerned the NGK's relationship with the Reformed Churches in the Netherlands and with the non-white 'daughter-churches'.

The name of each of the three Dutch Reformed Churches in South Africa is derived from that of an existing Dutch church. Since 1665 the NGK has been historically linked to the Gereformeerde Kerken in Nederland (Reformed Churches in the Netherlands), and the NHK (founded in 1853) to the Nederlandse Hervormde Kerk (Dutch Reformed Church). As members of the World Council of Churches these two Dutch churches have, since 1969, subscribed to the Fund for Liberation Movements

1. *Pro Veritate*, 15 October 1976, quoted in Goguel, op. cit., p. 102.

of the Special Fund to Combat Racism and have actively campaigned against apartheid. They have been particularly effective in mobilizing Dutch public opinion against investment in South Africa, and their campaign resulted, *inter alia*, in May 1976, in the withdrawal of the tender submitted by the Dutch-American consortium for the construction of the Koeberg nuclear power station. The contract was subsequently awarded to the French consortium Framatome.

In October 1974 the Fourth General Synod of the NGK, meeting at Cape Town, took the 'preliminary' decision to break with the Gereformeerde Kerken in Nederland, while leaving the 'final' decision to the next synod.

Meeting in Bloemfontein in October 1978, the Fifth General Synod approved this break almost unanimously, and thereby isolated the so-called Dutch Reformed churches of South Africa in the South African *laager* in which they had been born. The outcome of the vote was a foregone conclusion, and evoked little comment in the press, unlike three other resolutions dealing with South African domestic problems.

First, reverting to a long-standing discussion about the so-called biblical justification for the laws prohibiting racially mixed marriages (the 1927 Immorality Act and the 1950 and 1957 amendments to it), the synod retreated considerably from its original position. Whereas in 1974 'mixed' marriages had represented the 'destruction of the differentiation between the races ordained by God' and were 'forbidden by Holy Scripture', in 1978 these marriages were no longer 'impermissible' although they remained 'extremely undesirable'.[1]

Second, the synod refused two coloured candidates for ordination permission to attend the seminary set up by the NGK in the small town of Huguenot. This prohibition was in line with the last and by far the most important resolution of the synod, which should be set in its historical context in order to be understood.

We have seen that the NGK's missionary work had led to the establishment of three 'daughter churches' for the coloureds, the blacks and the Indians. These had separate buildings and a separate clergy, but were dependent in theological terms on the 'Mother Church', which organized them in a white-controlled federal council.

As early as in 1973 at the Federal council, a hundred black ministers of the NG Kerk in Afrika had vigorously denounced the flagrant injustice of a church that preached the Gospel of reconciliation to non-whites while simul-

1. *South African Digest*, 3 November 1978, p. 6.

taneously defending with all its might the exclusive privileges of the whites.

In 1974 the South African Council of Churches (SACC), comprising 13 million South African Christians, among them 12 million blacks, admitted as 'observer members' the three daughter churches of the NGK, representing (in 1970) 534,000 blacks, 549,000 coloureds and 1,300 Indians. As not one of the three Dutch Reformed Churches belonged to the SACC, this amounted to a frontal attack on the NGK's apartheid policy.

In 1975 the NG Kerk in Afrika changed its name to Black NGK in Africa and became a full member of the SACC.

At the meeting of the federal council in March 1978, the three daughter churches asked that the next NGK synod discuss their joint proposal to be represented by a single synod (Umbrella Synod). In September 1978 the coloured church, pursuing the drive for unification, asked for complete integration of the three daughter churches within each NGK congregation.

The 1978 synod rejected both these proposals, the one for a single synod and *a fortiori* the one for complete integration. It also rejected, by 210 votes to 206, an amendment suggesting that a commission be appointed 'to continue talks on unity'.

The following comments of the Afrikaans newspaper *Die Volksblad* would seem to represent the general state of mind of Afrikaners, who have been solely responsible for South African policy since 1948:

The Synod remains in favour of independent and ever more independent churches which are, in its view and experience, the test for the maintenance of good and also stronger family ties in the practical situation of the churches and their people in South Africa. This is a reality which would be dismissed in thought or wished away only to the detriment of the church's lofty calling. And this was in reality created by the King of the Church.[1]

'The South African racial situation was created by God.' That really is the Afrikaners' basic belief. Consequently any discussion with Afrikaners about South Africa's past or present is bound to lead to the conclusion: 'We are a chosen people entrusted with a divine mission, so all we have done and all we are doing is right.'

When intended for overseas consumption this statement is of course couched in more subtle terms, and most readers of the copious South African propaganda literature do not realize the crucial importance of the religious factor in the

1. *Die Volksblad,*
26 October 1978, translated in
South African Digest,
3 November 1978, p. 23.

current impasse of Pretoria's political thought. It is, however, a key factor, perhaps even more so today than before.

The few relaxations in petty apartheid, and even the envisaged abolition of the Immorality Act,[1] should not lead us to forget that in 1978 the Broederbond had about 11,000 members organized in 800 cells, 20 per cent of them teachers and 9 per cent clergymen. J. H. P. Serfontein, who gives these figures, emphasizes throughout his remarkable study[2] the close ties between the Afrikaner churches, the National Party (in power since 1948) and the Broederbond. The decisions of the 1978 NGK synod provide a recent illustration of this, as does the appointment in November 1978 of Dr Andries P. Treurnicht as leader of the National Party in the Transvaal.

A study of the Afrikaans churches is consequently a prerequisite to the understanding of the succeeding chapters.

1. In September 1979, in a statement violently attacked by the right wing of his party, Prime Minister Botha said he was ready to study proposals for modification of the laws forbidding marriage between persons of different races.
2. J. H. P. Serfontein, *Brotherhood of Power, An Exposé of the Secret Afrikaner Broederbond*, London, 1979.

Part Two:
Apartheid and the history of South African whites

4 History as seen by the Afrikaner

We may wonder why we invariably come across so many 'historical reminders' and 'historical justifications' in the speeches and writings of the advocates of apartheid. An indirect answer to this question was given in 1958 by the great Afrikaner historian F. A. van Jaarsveld, in an attempt to sum up the Afrikaner's notion of history: 'The Afrikaner's image of his past is based on national-political values and on biblical foundations. That is perhaps the reason for its ethical and moralizing note. . . .'[1]

The most essential of the 'national values' is undoubtedly love of freedom: 'The Boers saw their whole history as a struggle for freedom and independence.'[2]

In the Bible, the texts most charged with meaning are those that speak of the chosen people (of Israel), since the Afrikaners regard themselves as having been placed in Africa by God to fulfil a divine mission: 'It was Paul Kruger (1825–1904), President of the Transvaal between 1884 and 1900, who revealed God's leadership in the history of the Afrikaner people; whatever happened to them was His will; He was the Sovereign of history and its central theme.'[3]

Daniel François Malan (see the previous chapter) completely adopted this view of history, and expressed it in a famous passage: 'The history of the Afrikaner reveals a determination and a definiteness of purpose which make one feel that Afrikanerdom is not the work of man but a creation of God. We have a divine right to be Afrikaners. Our history is the highest work of art of the Architect of the centuries.'[4]

These ideas were reflected in a syllabus of 'Christian nationalist' teaching introduced in 1948 by a group of teachers at the Afrikaans University of Potchefstroom; it placed great emphasis on the teaching of 'national' history

. F. A. van Jaarsveld, *The Afrikaner's Interpretation of South African History*, translation of twelve lectures or articles in Afrikaans, Cape Town, 1964, p. 58.
. Ibid., p. 58.
. Ibid., p. 60.
. Quoted by Brian Bunting, *The Rise of the South African Reich*, 1964, p. 7.

as the best way of instilling love of country into children. The national history was, needless to say, the history of the Afrikaners, in which, according to van Jaarsveld, 'The Bantu has no real place other than as the foe during the Trekker and Republican periods, whilst the role assigned to the English-speaking is much more that of the persecutor of the Afrikaner than that of builder of the country.'[1]

Still according to van Jaarsveld, world history was treated extremely sketchily in Afrikaans textbooks until 1960,[2] whilst the history of mankind was taught exclusively according to the Bible and started with Genesis, no account being taken of advances in prehistoric anthropology.

Since 1960 a new and less restrictive syllabus has been introduced in school textbooks. But it should not be forgotten that the old textbooks were used by all Afrikaners of 40 and over, including every single politician to hold power in the 1970s. This explains the absolute impossibility of any historical discussion with an Afrikaner. An outsider raising an objection very quickly runs up against the wall of 'certainty' inculcated in school and reiterated in religious instruction.

The historical-religious amalgam

The fusion of Afrikaner history, Afrikaans language and Calvinist religion as taught in the three so-called Dutch Reformed Churches of South Africa was clearly expressed for the first time by Stephanus Jacob du Toit (1847–1911), an NGK minister from 1874 onwards, founder of the Genootskap van Regte Afrikaners (Fellowship of True Afrikaners) (1875), editor of the first Afrikaans newspaper, *Die Patriot*, and author of the first history book published in Afrikaans, *Die Geskiedenis van ons Land in die Taal van ons Volk* ('The History of Our Country in the Language of Our People').

The central concept is that God Himself placed the Afrikaners in Africa, that He Himself gave them the Afrikaans language, and that He entrusted them with a mission to spread Christian civilization in Africa. The main theme, however, is the Afrikaners' struggle, before and during the Great Trek, to defend their freedom against the 'English oppressors and persecutors'.

In his remarkable study on 'trends in South African historical writing in the nineteenth and twentieth centuries',[3] van Jaarsveld notes (and deplores) the persistence of this 'primarily anti-British' view of history held by Afrikaners until

1. Van Jaarsveld, op. cit., p. 66.
2. Ibid., p. 194.
3. Ibid., p. 116–65.

after the Second World War. This phenomenon explains the attitude of Lord Milner, who prohibited the teaching of history in schools after 1902 on the completely justifiable grounds that such teaching fostered the Afrikaners' nationalism (and hence their Anglophobia). Afrikaner mothers were at once enlisted to tell their children the great exploits of earlier generations. They naturally associated these with the Bible stories on which they and their parents and grandparents had been brought up.

Once again, as a result of Lord Milner's unwise decision the same fusion of history, language and religion recurs. It is hardly surprising that modern, more secular formulations of the Afrikaner ideology still bear its mark. For instance, in the introduction to his fascinating book *The Puritans in Africa*, devoted to the history of Afrikanerdom seen from the inside, W. A. de Klerk writes: 'We [the Afrikaners] are the instruments of Providence: or of History, which may well be a substitute for Providence.' A few lines later he states: 'The key to the Afrikaner is Calvinism.'[1]

In terms of the science of history in general, the historical-religious amalgam of the Afrikaners is of obvious interest. Throughout the world certain features of national ideologies and national myths supposedly originated from certain historical events that have generally been forgotten. Conversely, certain historical events are undoubtedly the direct or indirect consequence of the ruling ideology, but it is often difficult to establish the relationship of cause and effect. The relationship between ideology and historiography usually remains hypothetical.

In South Africa, on the other hand, both the small number and the isolation of the settlers during the formative period of the Afrikaner people and also the wealth of tradition at the time of the Great Trek provide the historian with a simplified, scaled-down model for the study of a universal phenomenon.

We shall now consider the history of South African whites from this particular angle, viz. its relationship to the ideology of apartheid.[2]

History as the source of ideology: the Dutch period (1652–1795)

1. W. A. de Klerk, *The Puritans in Africa*, London, 1975, p. xiii–xiv.
2. Several recent books about the history of South Africa are listed in the bibliography.

'Lost in Africa!' This was the title W. A. de Klerk gave to the first chapter of his book *The Puritans in Africa*, and it admirably expresses the drama that marked the formative period of the Afrikaner people and determined several features of the national ideology.

The striking feature of this 'Dutch period', which lasted from Jan van Riebeeck's landing on 6 April 1652 to the demise of the Dutch East India Company in 1795, is the very small number of colonists who settled on African soil and became 'white Africans' or Afrikaners speaking a new language called Afrikaans, in comparison with the colonists who settled in North America some decades earlier (1607 in Virginia, 1620 in Massachusetts) and became 'Americans' (while continuing to speak English). In 1780 the first census carried out in the United States showed a population of 3.2 million white Americans. In 1798 the Cape Colony, which had come under British administration three years earlier, comprised only 22,000 white Africans.

There are obviously many reasons to explain this enormous difference. First, there was the length of the voyage, which took twice as long to Cape Town as to Boston; but, above all, there was the authoritarian, governmental character of the Dutch East India Company, for which the only purpose of the 'victualling station' set up by Jan van Riebeeck in 1652 was to restock ships on the route to India. The company never developed a regular commercial service out of Cape Town. In 1707 it stopped the system of organized immigration, which in particular had been responsible in 1688 for bringing to the Cape 176 French Huguenots who had fled to Holland after the revocation of the Edict of Nantes. Its officials always kept tight control over the local government and refused to allow the settlers to take part in it.

Despite their small numbers (600 in 1679, 980 in 1694), the first Dutch, German and French settlers felt cramped in the Cape Peninsula, and looked for better farming land. They were lucky enough to come upon a well-watered, fertile area some twenty-five miles east of Cape Town. There the governor, Simon van de Stel, founded the town of Stellenbosch in 1679, and settled the French Huguenots. At the end of the Dutch period the Stellenbosch district had a population of 7,300, mostly farmers engaged in mixed farming (wheat, vines and fruit-trees) and cattle-raising.

As early as the beginning of the eighteenth century, the children of the Boers (farm labourers) left their fathers' farms in growing numbers to become *trekboers* (migratory stock-breeders). This was profitable because meat, which fetched a better price than grain, was taken to Cape Town markets on the hoof; it also gave them a definite psychological advantage, since they were much less at the mercy of the company's inspectors and controllers than the sedentary farmers. But the well-watered, fertile area of the Stellenbosch district is small—some 9,500 square kilometres; and 150 kilometres east of Cape Town the Karroo begins—a stunted semi-desert steppe where all that is possible is wide-ranging sheep-farming requiring long-distance movement. This type of vegetation, corresponding to a very low annual rainfall (less than 400 mm, and very irregular), extends 600 kilometres to the east (approximately to the latitude of Port Elizabeth) between the sea (except for a small strip of forest along the coast) and the Nieuwveld Range (about 230 kilometres from the coast) which formed the northern border of the Dutch Cape Colony.

These climatic and ecological features are of paramount importance. Indeed, it is necessary to know that the Karroo covered more than four-fifths of Cape Colony as defined by its 1786 borders, which remained unchanged until 1820. It is also necessary to know that, of the 22,000 Afrikaners recorded in the 1798 census, more than one-third, the 8,300 inhabitants of the 'new' eastern districts of Swellendam (founded in 1743) and Graaff-Reinet (founded in 1780), were *trekboers* of a very different stamp from the 7,300 sedentary Boers of the Stellenbosch district, and even more from the 6,300 town-dwelling burghers of the Cape district. For it was the descendants of the *trekboers*, not those of the Boers or burghers, who were to carry out the Great Trek, the heroic exploit of the Afrikaner people. And it is the extreme isolation of the eighteenth-century *trekboers*, lost in a hostile environment, that largely accounts for the extraordinary impact of the idea of a chosen people and a promised land, which, as we shall see, gave rise to some of the myths about South African blacks.

Before considering in greater detail the way of life of these eighteenth-century *trekboers*, the real founders of the Afrikaner nation, we must revert to the racial stratification of South African society upon which the apartheid doctrine was built and which originated in the early days of the Dutch period.

In 1658, five years after Jan van Riebeeck's landing, the arrival at the Cape of an early convoy of slaves made it clear once and for all that manual work was the province of the non-whites, whether slaves or Hottentots (Khoikhoi). According to the 1798 census there were 26,000 slaves, nine-tenths of whom lived in the two 'old' districts of the Cape and Stellenbosch, and 15,000 'Hottentot servants', 14,000 of them in the two 'new' districts of Swellendam and especially

Graaff-Reinet. Thus 22,000 white masters had an average of two non-white servants apiece.

By the end of the nineteenth century the relationship between masters and servants had not changed at all, but the 39,000 slaves freed in 1834 had been integrated, together with many Hottentots, into the coloured 'racial group', and pure-blooded Hottentots survived only in very small numbers. The white masters were both Afrikaners and English-speakers; the non-white servants were now mostly blacks (Bantu), except in the Cape Province, where the coloureds were in a majority.

This change in the composition of the multiracial society in South Africa is generally misunderstood, and few people realize that life in the Dutch colony at the Cape went on in a racial context very different from that of today.

The Hottentots (Khoi) and Bushmen (San), grouped together in modern ethnological language as the Khoisan, were the only aborigines of the Cape as defined by its 1795 frontiers. They were not Negroes (Bantu). Their skin was a dull yellowish colour, their features mongoloid with high, prominent cheek-bones, and their hair was sparse and of the so-called peppercorn type. Their language used the quite specific consonants known as 'clicks'. The Khoisan physical type and language today survive in a pure state only among the San hunters (an estimated 50,000 in number), who lead a nomadic existence in the Kalahari desert in Namibia and Botswana, and among the Khoikhoi (Nama) (37,000 in 1974) of Namibia.

While the Cape burghers and the Stellenbosch Boers had slaves as servants, the *trekboers* mainly used Hottentots. The latter's tribal structure was completely disrupted by two big smallpox epidemics in 1713 and 1755. Apart from some localized revolts, the survivors integrated into white society (always as servants) or left the Cape colony in organized groups, like the Nama, who emigrated to what is now Namibia, or the Griqua, a mixture of 'Cape bastards' (born in the seventeenth century of white fathers and Hottentot mothers) and Griqua Hottentots, who left in 1775 for the confluence of the Orange and Vaal rivers.

On the other hand, the Bushmen (San) hunters remained strong until the end of the eighteenth century, owing to their extraordinary mobility. Continually attacking isolated *trekboers*, they were themselves savagely hunted down. In 1774 a 250-man Boer commando with Hottentot auxiliaries killed over 5,000 of them and took 240 prisoners on a single expedition.[1] The savagery of the repression is to be explained

1. E. A. Walker, *A History o[f] Southern Africa*, 1904, p. 97.

by the *trekboers'* fear of their elusive, ubiquitous enemy, a feeling intensified by their own isolation.

Isolation is undoubtedly the most significant single factor in the development of the Afrikaner national character. It affected the whole of white society during the Dutch period. Even the people of the Cape saw few ships calling and had few visitors who stayed long enough to enrich their lives culturally. In 1778 there were only three secondary or 'high-school' institutions (including a private 'French school').[1] The Boers (farmers) of the Stellenbosch district were scattered in inaccessible valleys, and rarely went to the capital.

Although they seldom saw outsiders, the Cape burghers and Stellenbosch Boers had no difficulty meeting at church. The situation was very different for the *trekboers*. Those who lived in the east of the colony travelled several weeks to get to the nearest church for the *Nachtmaal* (Holy Communion) celebrations. A young couple from Bruyntjeshoogte, in what is now the Somerset East region, had to make a three-month journey to get married at the Cape and return home. Even visits to neighbours were difficult, since farms were so extensive. Under a system used until about 1820, they were demarcated by riding on horseback for half an hour in each direction of the compass from a central point fixed by the future owner. This resulted in properties of 7,500 acres or more.

Apart from the *Nachtmaal* gatherings the daily service conducted by the head of the household and attended by masters and servants alike was the only cultural feature in the *trekboers'* lives. It was the only spiritual recourse strengthening them in their fight against the wild animals, the elusive Bushmen hunters and the generally hostile environment.

The well-known saying 'the Boer with his Bible in one hand and his rifle in the other' which was to symbolize the heroes of the Great Trek, is a direct result of the lives led by the eighteenth-century *trekboers*.

These nomadic stock-breeders, nurtured solely on the Bible, paid special attention to the accounts of the Hebrews' long march to Palestine, and thought that the vast wilderness of the Karroo, scoured by several generations of *trekboers*, would also lead to a promised land. It is hardly surprising that they reacted as they did when they finally reached the lush meadows between the Sunday and Great Fish Rivers and found them already occupied by Xhosa herdsmen. It seemed obvious that the Xhosa were the Philistines settled in Palestine when the Hebrews arrived and equally obvious

1. De Klerk, op. cit., p. 7.

that they, the 'chosen people', had every right to drive the blacks out of the land promised to the whites. The same deep conviction of right was to characterize all their subsequent encounters with the blacks.

All the essential features of Afrikaner ideology—a racially stratified society, love of independence (a reaction against the authoritarianism of the Dutch East India Company), land hunger, a taste for geographical separation (with the border fixed at Fish River in 1778), and the idea of the chosen people—all were determined by the historical and geographical conditions during the Dutch period.

Ideology as the source of history

We shall confine ourselves to two particularly illuminating examples: the Great Trek and the national holiday of 16 December.

The causes of the Great Trek

The chapter on history in *South Africa 1977* summarizes the Great Trek as follows:

This migration, the Great Trek of 1835–37, by Boer frontier farmers, the *Voortrekkers*, was a deliberate move by thousands of men and women who left hearth and home in their ox-wagons at great personal sacrifice to put as much distance as possible between themselves and a British government at the Cape. The Great Trek was indeed a turning-point in South African history, and one of the greatest single events of the nineteenth century.[1]

While it may be an exaggeration to regard the Great Trek as one of the greatest single events of world history in the nineteenth century, its general historical interest is undeniable. Today, when many historians concern themselves exclusively with economics and statistics, the Great Trek is a striking example of the power of ideologies.

South Africa, an official publication intended for overseas readers, gives no further information about the charges levelled at the Cape government. But school textbooks set out at length the grievances of the 'frontier farmers', and quote documents written by the Voortrekkers themselves, including Piet Retief's *Manifesto*, published on 22 January 1837 in an English translation in the *Grahamstown Journal* (Grahamstown is the town around which the

1. *South Africa 1977*, p. 42.

4,000 British colonists who arrived in 1820 settled), and Anna Steenkamp's *Diary*.

After devoting twenty pages to British policy towards the non-whites between 1806 and 1836, a Standard-8 textbook summarizes the 'causes of the Great Trek' in three pages under three headings. First, British policy towards the non-whites—Hottentots, slaves and Xhosa blacks—takes up two pages, with special emphasis on the disastrous consequences of Ordinance 50 of 1828, which gave the Hottentots the same civic rights as whites. Secondly, six 'other causes' take up less than a page (particular mention should be made of the replacement of the Dutch in the administration by the English and the frontier farmers' land hunger). Thirdly, the five-line conclusion perfectly illustrates the title of this chapter:

We may distinguish two threads which run through the above reasons for the dissatisfaction of the Boers with the British government: (a) British policies threatened their fundamental traditions—they were being wounded spiritually; (b) British policies caused them such losses that their material well-being was in jeopardy.[1]

In her diary Anna Steenkamp explained the nature of this assault on the Voortrekkers' fundamental traditions:

And yet it was not their [the non-whites'] freedom that drove us to such lengths, as their being placed on an equal footing with Christians, contrary to the laws of God and the natural distinction of race and religion, so that it was intolerable for any decent Christian to bow down beneath such a yoke, wherefore we rather withdrew in order to preserve our doctrines in purity.[2]

Piet Retief wrote in his *Manifesto*: 'It is our determination . . . to preserve proper relations between master and servant.'[3] 'Proper relations' means that the white is always the master and that the master (*baas*) is always a white. A non-white cannot by definition be anything but a servant.

The application of this principle resulted in the famous clause that in 1858 was written into the constitution of the first Zuid-Afrikaansche Republiek of the Transvaal: 'The people are not prepared to allow any equality of the non-white with the white inhabitants, either in church or state.' By establishing the 'definitive' civil and religious inferiority of the non-whites, this clause, as we have seen, constitutes the essential prerequisite for the doctrine of apartheid.

1. *Senior Secondary History for Standard Eight*, 1974, p. 116.
2. J. Bird (ed.), *The Annals of Natal 1495 to 1845*, Pietermaritzburg, 1888, p. 459.
3. De Klerk, op. cit., p. 23. The complete text of the *Manifesto* is given on p. 22–4.

The national holiday of 16 December

Geloftedag (Day of the Covenant) commemorates the appeal
to the Almighty on 9 December 1838 by a commando of
464 men under the orders of Andries Pretorius. For the 4,000
or so Voortrekkers who wanted to settle in Natal this
commando was really the last chance: on 6 February 1838
the Zulu king Dingaan had had their leader Piet Retief put
to death, together with 70 white comrades and 30 coloured
servants, and in the ensuing months some 250 whites and as
many coloureds.

Seven days after Pretorius's men had solemnly vowed
that they and their descendants would observe an annual
day of thanksgiving if God granted them victory, they
met 10,000 Zulu warriors on the banks of the little river
Ncome (a sub-tributary of the Tugela). After some hours
of shooting from their laager of fifty-seven wagons, they
had killed 3,000 Zulu: the blood stained the water of the
river, which is known to this day as Blood River. The
Voortrekkers had only two casualties, neither of them fatal.

Considering the enormous disparity of the two forces,
it is quite understandable that such a signal victory, coming
after so many tribulations, should have been ascribed to the
Covenant entered into with God.

But divine protection was less apparent when in 1843 the
British annexed the Republic of Natal (proclaimed in 1839)
and forced the Trekkers to introduce a policy of racial
equality. The majority of the Trekkers then went back over
the Drakensberg passes to get into the interior (Transvaal
and Orange Free State) where land was still available and
they could re-establish 'proper' relations between whites
and non-whites.

In 1864, 16 December was proclaimed NGK day in
Natal, and in 1865 the Transvaalers proclaimed 16 December
a public holiday under the name *Dingaan's Dag* (Dingaan's
Day).

On 16 December 1867 a great religious celebration with
the reconstitution of the 1838 laager was held at the actual
site of the battle. But the commemoration of the vow of
9 December 1838 took on its full significance only after
the British annexation of the Transvaal on 12 April 1877.

On 9 December 1880 some 9,000 armed burghers
assembled at Paardekraal (near what is now Krugersdorp)
and vowed to fight for the recovery of Transvaal's independence (Transvaal had been independent between 1852
and 1877). On 16 December the *Vierkleur*, or national flag,

was hoisted in the town of Heidelberg, which had been chosen as the seat of the future government. This was the beginning of the First War of Independence.

On 27 February 1881 a commando of 75 Boers routed a detachment of 700 British at Majuba Hill at a cost of one killed and five wounded, and the Transvaal regained its independence. It was at first partial independence under the Pretoria Convention of 1881, and then full independence under the London Convention of 1884.

At Majuba Hill, just as at Blood River, the disparity of forces overwhelmingly favoured the Boers' enemies and victory was again ascribed to divine intervention.

Against this background it is understandable that the vow of 9 December 1838 should have been solemnly renewed before and during the *Tweede Vryheidsoorlog* (Second War of Independence), better known abroad as the Boer War (1899–1902). Its extraordinary impact on the Boers' fighting spirit so impressed the British that Lord Milner had the cairn raised at Paardekraal on 9 December 1880 demolished and the stones taken to Durban, where they were thrown into the sea.[1]

The new cairn raised at Nooitgedacht in the Transvaal on 16 December 1900 did not bring the Boers victory. But far from losing confidence in divine protection after 1902, the Boers observed 16 December with even greater fervour. President Kruger, who had died in Switzerland, was buried at Pretoria on 16 December 1904 and, in 1910, 16 December was proclaimed a public holiday at the first session of the Union Parliament. The Women's Monument erected in Pretoria in memory of the thousands of Boer women who died in British concentration camps in 1901–02 was dedicated on 16 December 1913.

On 16 December 1938 the foundation stone of the Voortrekkers' Monument in Pretoria was laid, and it was officially dedicated on 16 December 1949 in the presence of a crowd estimated at 250,000 people, or one Afrikaner in six. Such attendance, in a country where distances are great and at a time when domestic air travel was in its infancy, shows how responsive Afrikaners were to the message of 16 December.

In the same year a long-standing request of the Afrikaans Churches was granted when the name *Dingaan's Dag* was replaced by *Geloftedag*, which better recalled the essentially religious significance of the early commemorations.

After their success in the 1948 elections, and particularly with the proclamation of the Republic in 1961, the Afrikaners

1. W. Kistner, 'The 16th of December in the Context of Nationalist Thinking', in *Church and Nationalism in South Africa*, Ravan Press, 1975.

were entitled to suppose that they had won on all fronts
without the necessity of a 'Third War of Independence',
which had been commonly expected after the Boer War. But
they still did not dream of giving up the celebration of
16 December. Interest now focused mainly on the laager,
the encampment made up of wagons placed in a circle that
played a decisive role in the battle of Blood River.

.And, as the pressure of black Africa on white Africa
mounts, the idea of the whites withdrawing into the laager
gains ground in certain Afrikaner circles. The South African
Government has not reacted passively. It has planned several
major public works projects in Cape Province to the west of
the Ciskei, with the obvious aim of making this area, which
may be regarded as the Afrikaners' real historic homeland
(see the following chapter), a viable economic entity.

Once more ideology has been a source of history.

Discussion of the historical arguments that 'justify' the white homeland

To justify the extremely unjust land distribution (87 per cent
of the total area of South Africa reserved for 16 per cent of
the total population), official South African literature relies
essentially on historical arguments.

The overall position is summarized in the following
quotations from Chapter 12 of *South Africa 1977*. The first
comes from the beginning of the account of the 'Geographical
Bases of Multinational Development':

History has over more than three centuries delineated South
Africa into distinct ethnic homelands. Their geographical distribution is the physical basis for the present-day geopolitical
relations between the homeland of the white nation (the RSA)
and those of the principal black peoples within the boundaries
of South Africa.[1]

The second quotation introduces the 'Realities of the South
African Situation': 'The first reality is that the whites will
only be able to maintain their national identity as long as they
control their own political destiny in that part of South Africa
which history has given them as their homeland, namely
the RSA.'[2]

The historical arguments are listed in Chapter 4, 'The
Peoples of South Africa': 'White South Africa (The Republic
of South Africa—RSA) includes those parts historically

1. *South Africa 1977*, p. 205.
2. Ibid., p. 211.

occupied, settled and developed by the whites.'[1] A few lines further on the writer develops this statement:

Historically, white South Africans are an African people. They base their claim on the realities of both past and contemporary history. This claim may be synthesised into the combined realities of, first, effective and historically continuous occupation and habitation; secondly, continuous and historically sustained development and thirdly, effective and historically uninterrupted political control.[2]

Chapter 12, 'Multinational Development', repeats virtually the same phrases in a shorter form and adds two new arguments: 'the progressive determining of boundaries' and 'the evolution of a language significantly named Afrikaans'.[3]

Before discussing each of the five historical arguments, it must first be pointed out that while the history of white Afrikaans-speaking South Africans (60 per cent of the white population) began over three centuries ago, that of English-speaking white South Africans (37 per cent of the white population) goes back only a century and a half. The few English people who came to South Africa between 1795 (the year of the first British occupation) and 1820 did not settle there; and it is the establishment of 4,000 British settlers in the Grahamstown area in 1820 that marks the real beginning of the history of English-speaking South Africans. Here, then, we encounter the first instance of dishonesty, namely the application of historical arguments to the 'white nation' or 'white South Africans' where 'white' means only Afrikaner.

Even admitting this first fallacy, are the arguments advanced elsewhere valid?

The territory of the white homeland is defined by effective, continuous, historical (white) occupation.

South Africa 1977 makes it quite clear that occupation for over three centuries is what is meant: 'The whites of the RSA today rightfully define themselves as a permanently established African nation geopolitically rooted in a part of the continent which in the course of more than three centuries has become their only fatherland.[4] This quotation should be taken together with the following one, which is continually repeated in political speeches and writings. For example, in 1975 Eschel Rhoodie, then Secretary for Information, stated: 'Neither the blacks nor the whites have a prior claim to the whole of South Africa. Each owns the territories they occupied first.'[5]

A significant variant of this assertion is set out in *South Africa 1977*. The beginning is the same, but the second

1. Ibid., p. 76.
2. Ibid.
3. Ibid., p. 209.
4. Ibid., p. 208.
5. *Le Monde*, Tribune Internationale, 12 August 1975.

sentence reads: 'Neither the whites nor any of the black nations have a prior claim to all of South Africa. Each has such a claim only to that part which history has given it as a homeland.'[1]

A territory genuinely and continuously occupied for three centuries; a territory occupied first (in relation to the blacks): a part, but only a very small part of the present white homeland (the RSA) fits this historical definition, namely the Dutch colony at the Cape within the borders set for it in 1778 (eastern border set at Great Fish River) and 1781 (when the northern border of the new District of Graaff-Reinet was settled). We have seen that within this territory of 170,000 square kilometres, or 14 per cent of the total area of present-day South Africa, the Khoisan native peoples were of a physical type quite different from the blacks (Bantu).

But beyond the Orange River, i.e. in the three provinces of Orange Free State, Transvaal and Natal, this definition is inapplicable. The very first whites (British and Americans) to settle in Natal arrived in 1824. The Voortrekkers, who joined them only in 1837, did not stay in Natal and were replaced (only from 1849 onwards) by British colonists. In the Orange Free State, the first permanent settlements of trekboers date from 1830; the Voortrekkers arrived in 1836. The same is true of the Transvaal, where there were practically no whites before 1835. In short, 1835 marks the beginning of white occupation of the three provinces beyond the Orange River, where the major part of South Africa's economic power is concentrated. Almost two centuries—183 years—separate 1835 from 1652, the date which Afrikaners unfailingly cite to demonstrate their long-standing presence in Africa.

If we look at the other end of Africa, we find that in 1962 history undid what the French did in Algeria five years before 1835. The relatively short duration of European occupation outside the southern part of Cape Province suggests that South African whites, both Afrikaners and English-speakers, could well find themselves one day in the same situation as the French in Algeria after 1954.

'The territory of the white homeland is defined by continuous and historically sustained development.' Nobody would dream of denying the major role of the whites in the remarkable economic development of South Africa. Considering, however, that the Afrikaners ('who have no other country') are primarily concerned with justifying their privileges on historical grounds, it is somewhat ironic that they employ this argument. In their 'true' homeland, the southern

1. *South Africa 1977*, p. 21(

Cape Province, merino sheep, the Karroo's only real asset, were introduced only in 1827—by the English. Before 1870, when diamonds were discovered, the Boer republics of the Orange Free State and Transvaal were largely barter economies and had only a very limited number of schools. Clergymen, schoolteachers and politicians' secretaries were recruited in Europe. The country's few business men were largely of British origin.

President Kruger's opinions about the activities of the gold-digging *Uitlanders* (foreigners) are well known, and were summarized by General Louis Botha, who said in 1902, before the Treaty of Vereeniging: 'Independence must be safeguarded, even at the cost of giving up the whole of the Rand, for these gold-fields are the cancer of the country.'

The Afrikaners' economic breakthrough is real but extremely recent. It is therefore difficult in their case to speak of 'continuous development through history'.

'The territory of the homeland is defined by effective and historically uninterrupted political control.' As in the economic argument, we need to know to whom we are referring. If it is the whites in general, the statement is tenable. But the term 'historically uninterrupted' is not appropriate if we are talking about the Afrikaners alone or the English alone. The Transvaal, for example, was recognized in 1852, was then annexed by the British in 1877, and became independent again in 1881, at the end of the First War of Independence.

'The progressive determining of boundaries' is the fourth argument in support of the 'claims of the white nation to national existence on African soil'.[1] Anyone who has not been raised in the mould of the Afrikaner mentality will find it difficult to understand the relationship of cause and effect here. There is no need to dwell on it.

'The evolution of a new language significantly named Afrikaans' is stressed. One of the weaknesses of this argument is that it applies only to the Afrikaners and not to the entire white nation. While undoubtedly respectable, it would certainly be much more so if white Afrikaans-speakers (the Afrikaners) did justice to 'brown' Afrikaans-speakers (the coloureds); for the latter's ancestors were largely responsible for changing the Dutch spoken by the first seventeenth-century settlers into a new language. But despite the almost religious reverence the Afrikaners feel for their language, the coloureds are victims of apartheid and are deprived of all political rights at the national level in South Africa.

1. *South Africa 1977*, p. 209.

Conclusion

The white homeland today occupies 87 per cent of what was the total area of South Africa before the 'independence' of the Transkei and Bophuthatswana. It contains 67 per cent of the total population and produces more than 90 per cent of the national income (in 1975).

The true white homeland, historically speaking, namely the Dutch Cape Colony, would occupy 14 per cent of the total area. It would contain less than 20 per cent of the population, and would produce less than 20 per cent of the national income.

Obviously a great deal is at stake in this argument. That is why the advocates of apartheid take such pains to discover historical justifications.

But this type of argument seems to be reserved particularly for foreigners. To Afrikaner audiences, conditioned by the teaching of school and church, speakers still invoke the idea of 'divine right', as in this passage from a speech given (in Afrikaans) on 5 November 1974 by J. B. Vorster, then Prime Minister:

I made it very clear to the world that we assuredly have the right to say that we are as much a part of Africa as any other country in Africa. But even more clearly have I stressed that we are not here in Africa by virtue of the grace of anybody, but we are here in Africa by virtue of our right to be here.[1]

Any comment on this profession of faith seems superfluous; let it serve as a conclusion to the discussion of the justification of the white homeland.

1. F. R. Metrovich (ed.), *Towards Dialogue and Déten* 1975, p. 33–4.

Part Three:
Apartheid and the history
of South African blacks

5 South African ethnic groups and 'nations'

In South Africa, the meaning of the terms 'ethnic groups' and 'nations' varies according to whether one is speaking of blacks or whites.

Despite the great differences between English and Afrikaans, the whites are officially presented as a single white nation, i.e. defined solely by skin colour.

By contrast, the much smaller differences between the languages spoken by the Africans (particularly between the languages in the Nguni group and those in the Sotho group spoken by 93 per cent of black South Africans) are the major criterion for the definition of 'nine separate ethnic groups, each with its own language, legal system, life style, values and socio-political identity'.[1] 'Each of the nine groups is a potential independent nation and is being developed with the assistance of the white nation.'[2]

Although the specificity of each of the nine South African ethnic groups is presented as self-evident, the foreign reader cannot help wondering about the obvious advantage to the white minority of dividing the black majority into nine separate political groupings. Isn't this division of the blacks into nine 'emergent nations' simply a pseudo-scientific way of camouflaging the principle common to all colonial powers, namely divide and rule?

That, at any rate, is the conclusion an objective observer reaches after a close look at the supposedly wide linguistic and socio-political disparities of the various ethnic groups.

1. *South Africa 1977*, p. 82.
2. Ibid., p. 87.

The so-called linguistic identities
of the nine black 'nations'

In fact there are not nine linguistic groups in South Africa but four. Moreover, this is clearly stated in *South Africa 1977*: 'The major group of southern Bantu is subdivided into four main cultural-linguistic groups, namely the Nguni, Sotho-Tswana, Venda and Shangaan-Tsonga. These subdivisions are based principally on historical, linguistic and cultural differences.'[1]

The official publication is careful, however, not to give figures in this general description. This is a pity, for since the Venda and Shangaan-Tsonga groups together make up only 7 per cent of South African blacks, it would be fair to say that there are really only two main linguistic groups in South Africa, the Nguni group and the Sotho group.

The Nguni group in 1976 comprised over 10 million people, or 57 per cent of South African blacks and more than twice the number of white South Africans.

The four languages of the Nguni group—Zulu, Xhosa, Swazi and Ndebele—share 70 per cent of their vocabulary and are therefore mutually intelligible to a very large degree and much more so than Afrikaans and English. Moreover, some subgroups such as the Pondo, who live in the northern half of the Transkei, claim to be of Zulu origin and yet speak Xhosa. This being so, the foreign observer finds it difficult to understand the 'grand design' of apartheid, which entails creating not four but five black 'nations' from these four dialects of the Nguni language.

The Xhosa (or Cape Nguni) form not one 'nation' but two: the Transkei, which became 'independent' on 26 October 1976 (with a population of more than 4 million in 1976, 1,760,000 of whom live in the white homeland, where they are regarded as foreigners) and the Ciskei (with a population of 870,000, less than half of whom live within the homeland).

The Zulu (or Natal Nguni) were estimated at over 5 million in 1976, and represent the biggest ethnic group in South Africa, outnumbering the Xhosa and also the whites (4.3 million in 1976).

Chief Gatsha Buthelezi rejected the 'independence' of Kwa Zulu, which was fragmented into ten pieces under the 'final' regrouping bill of 1975, though this was a great advance on the 113 separate fragments of which the country was made up in 1978. The numerical preponderance of Zulu in the industrial areas of Johannesburg and especially of

1. *South Africa 1977*, p. 82.

Durban (31 per cent of Soweto's population is Zulu, and 91 per cent of that of the townships around Durban) means that Zulu is becoming the lingua franca of a large part of the urbanized Africans in white areas. For example, despite the predominance of Sotho-speakers among the miners (because many of them come from Lesotho), the Zulu vocabulary predominates in Fanakalo, an artificial language based on English, Afrikaans and Zulu that is systematically taught to all miners.

The Swazi, estimated at 590,000 in 1976, have a homeland of the same name adjoining independent Swaziland (which had an estimated population of only 528,000 in 1976). Less than 20 per cent of South African Swazi live in this homeland.

The Southern Ndebele (240,000 in 1976), who speak a language closely related to Zulu, have been allocated (so far only on paper) a homeland of 750 sq. km in the northern Transvaal, which makes them the tenth 'black nation' and completely invalidates the official doctrine that an ethnic group is defined by its language. For the northern Ndebele speak the Pedi language of the northern Sotho, while other Ndebele 'tribes' speak Tswana. But these three groups speaking different languages have a common history that links them to the Swazi. An amusing aspect of this effort to present a single ethnic group as belonging to three linguistic groups is the detailed description in *South Africa 1977*:

A Nguni offshoot, often confused with the North Sotho are the Ndebele of the Transvaal. They have no historical connection with the Ndebele in Matabeleland (Rhodesia), who are better known as the Matabele. . . . The Ndebele proper are an ancient tribe, related to the Swazi and Hlubi, who also moved from the Natal interior to the central eastern Transvaal, i.e. east of Pretoria. The northern Transvaal Ndebele have acculturated considerably to the Northern Sotho and speak mainly the Pedi language. Other Ndebele tribes have acculturated completely to the Tswana and can speak only Setswana. Two branches have retained their culture and language similar to Zulu.[1]

The Sotho group numbered 6 million speakers in 1976. It comprises three subgroups, whose close kinship is shown by the names Northern Sotho, Southern Sotho and Western Sotho or Tswana.

The Northern Sotho or Bapedi are the largest group, and were estimated at 2.2 million in 1976, less than half of whom lived in the Lebowa homeland (made up of seven fragments) in the northern Transvaal.

2.1 million Tswana (or Western Sotho) are the 'citizens'

1. Ibid., p. 86.

of Bophuthatswana, which has been 'independent' since 6 December 1977 and is also made up of seven parts, three of which are in north-west Transvaal, three in the northern Cape Province (formerly British Bechuanaland) and one in the Orange Free State (600 kilometres from the other closest fragment). It is estimated that one third of the resident population (thought to be 1.2 million in 1976) is non-Tswana—a flagrant contradiction of the principle that each black 'nation' must be composed of only one ethnic group.

The Southern Sotho, estimated at 1.7 million in 1976, have a homeland called Qwaqwa in the Orange Free State north of Lesotho only 480 sq. km large: in short, an area of 0.3 sq. km per 1,000 Southern Sotho (see Table 2, p. 27). This being so, it is not surprising that 93 per cent of the Southern Sotho have settled in white areas or in other homelands such as the Transkei.

This brief account of the main linguistic groups shows that the concept of 'linguistic identity' needs to be revised in South Africa much more than in most countries of black Africa—which, it should be noted, are with rare exceptions pluri-ethnic and generally comprise more than nine ethnic groups.

For three reasons, South Africa is a linguistic conglomeration that would lend itself particularly to the use of one national language throughout the country. First, it belongs to the block of Bantu-speaking countries (which broadly covers Africa south of the equator), and everyone, including the authors of *South Africa 1977*, takes the view that 'the Bantu languages form a more coherent and perhaps more compact language family than any other in the world'.[1] Second, common Nguni and common Sotho, spoken by 93 per cent of all black South Africans, bear the same relationship to each other as French and Italian. Third, the differences between the languages of the Nguni group or of the Sotho group are, to quote *South Africa 1977* once again, 'generally minor and do not constitute any very great barrier to mutual intelligibility'.[2]

Instead of fostering the natural inclination of South Africans to use a common African language, the Pretoria Government does everything it can to re-create nine linguistic groups. Accordingly, the mother tongue is the compulsory medium of instruction in township schools in white areas, not only during the first three years (as is done all over Africa and particularly in the homelands) but throughout primary school up to and including Standard 5.

1. *South Africa 1977*, p. 105.
2. Ibid., p. 105.

The so-called socio-political identities
of the nine black 'nations'

If the identity of each of the nine black 'nations' is debatable
from a linguistic standpoint, so it is equally questionable from
a socio-political point of view.

We have seen the example of the Ndebele of the Transvaal,
who 'acculturated' to the Northern Sotho or the Tswana
(Western Sotho), while a minority, the Southern Ndebele, kept
the Swazi (Nguni) language and culture of the original group.

Examples of contemporary ethnic groups claiming both
Sotho and Nguni origin are many. The best-known is that
of the Basuto 'nation' founded by the great King Moshweshwe
(died 1870), who brought together the Sotho and Nguni tribes
in the Lesotho mountains.

The two smallest linguistic groups are also far from being
as individualized as official doctrine claims. For instance,
the Shangaan-Tsonga of Gazankulu (near Mozambique)
have incorporated Sotho and Venda clans.

Certain ethnic groups such as the Zulu and the Tswana
show a remarkable ability to integrate, which is no doubt
due to the close kinship between the various South African
Bantu languages. We shall revert to the example of the Zulu
in succeeding chapters. Here we may mention that of the
Tswana, as set out in the highly official *Standard Encyclopaedia of Southern Africa* in its five-page article by F. J. Language on the Western Sotho: 'An outstanding feature of the
Tswana is the fact that the tribe generally has a particularly
heterogeneous composition nowadays. A Tswana tribe is
often composed of groups that differ radically as regards
language, customs, traditions, descent and ethnic affinities.'
After giving several examples, the author continues: 'Citi-
zenship or membership in the tribe among the Tswana is not
limited; it is available to every person of good conduct and
character who wishes to settle in the tribal area, provided he
has the approval of the tribal chief.'[1]

The reader will have noted that the idea of groups that
'differ radically as regards language, customs, traditions,
descent and ethnic affinities' within the same tribe explicitly
contradict the official statements quoted at the beginning of
this chapter.

While there is no question here of denying the differences
between the various linguistic groups in South Africa, it is
fair to say that they are just like others all over the world,
in black, yellow and white countries, and that they do not

1. *Standard Encyclopaedia
of Southern Africa*, Vol. 10,
p. 74, Cape Town, 1974.

preclude similarities. The Pretoria Government is aware of this, since *South Africa 1977* devotes six pages to 'traditional Bantu society' as a whole and only four to all the various linguistic groups.

The so-called homogeneity of the white nation

The insistence of theorists of apartheid on dividing the blacks into nine nations (actually ten, counting the homeland of the Southern Ndebele) thus seems suspect, the more since the whites themselves are far from being a single homogeneous nation.

Before their recent joining of forces in a white South African nationalism, the two groups which constitute the white nation had fought each other for a hundred and fifty years. The history of the Afrikaners is essentially that of their struggle against the British. Its most conspicuous features are the Great Trek, directed against the British administration, and the two Wars of Independence (1880–81 and 1899–1902) against British imperialism. The Boers' physical defeat in 1902 was compensated for by their 'moral victory' and by the worldwide condemnation of the British concentration camps, in which more than 25,000 Boer women and children perished.

Such things are not forgotten in one generation, and the awkwardness that persists between Afrikaans and English-speaking South Africans is noticeable in several passages in *South Africa 1977*. Having explained that the two Wars of Independence waged by the Boers against the British represent the beginning of the decolonization of the African continent, the writer continues:

Over the years, Afrikaner nationalism has gradually broadened into a more comprehensive white South African nationalism, embracing also the aspirations of the vast majority of South Africans of British stock with whom the Afrikaners share the basic tenets of Western civilization. It is particularly in the current decade that this process has become manifest. Between those of British stock and their Afrikaner compatriots there has been a growing comradeship, a new identity of purpose, a genuine sentiment of shared nationhood.[1]

These words mean simply that Afrikaner nationalism has emerged from an anti-British into an anti-African phase. The enemy has changed, but not the ideology. There is no

1. *South Africa 1977*, p. 80.

question of the Afrikaners giving up their language or their culture. Nor is there any question of English-speaking South Africans becoming full-fledged Afrikaners, even the few who have a complete command of Afrikaans.

The present educational system exaggerates the linguistic and cultural separation of the two sections of the white community, since schools and universities are unilingual, with the exception of the University of Port Elizabeth.[1] (In schools, the other language is taught as a compulsory subject from Standard 3 upwards.)

In practice one meets many Afrikaners and few English-speaking South Africans who are perfectly bilingual. Despite claims for its unity, the white community will continue to be characterized by two languages, two cultures and two histories. According to the official definitions of the nine black nations, it should therefore be divided into two nations. It will be said—and rightly—that this would be to swim against the tide of history. It is all the more true of the effort of the Pretoria Government to divide South African blacks artificially into nine nations.

1. Established in terms of the Act of 1964. Total enrolment was 2,700 in 1977.

Falsifications of South African history up to 1936: ten myths and their refutations

6 Myth I

*That the whites and the blacks
arrived in South Africa
at the same time*

The subtitle of this chapter, which is presented as a positive fact in official South African literature, represents a major historical falsification.

Twenty years ago it was scientifically proved that the blacks came first. Recent carbon-14 datings show that Bantu-speaking peoples, ancestors of the South African blacks, settled in the northern Transvaal in the third century, i.e. 1,400 years before the whites established themselves at the Cape.

South African historians, who know well that the blacks came first, have never intervened to have the official doctrine altered. Even though it is sometimes expressed in an attenuated form, the theory of simultaneous migrations of whites and blacks is still upheld nowadays in political speeches and recently published school textbooks. Still more serious, it has been defended so long and so vigorously that it has been uncritically repeated, even very recently, by foreign authors.

Various domestic and foreign versions of this great myth of South African history will be presented in the first part of this chapter. The second part, devoted to the refutation of the myth, will present a summary of our current knowledge about the black settlement of South Africa in the first millennium A.D.

Various versions of the myth

By South Africans

As in the subsequent chapters, *South Africa 77*, published by the now-defunct Department of Information, will be quoted first: 'Prior to their southward migration the forebears of the present black groups apparently used to live in the region of the great lakes of Central Africa. Their entry into what is today South Africa roughly coincided with the arrival of the first whites at the Cape in 1652.'[1]

Another of the Department of Information's publications gives a more detailed account:

In the 1770's, some one thousand kilometres to the north-east of Cape Town, the Afrikaner migratory stream came into substantial contact with the vanguard of a second migratory movement from the vicinity of the Great Lakes of Central Africa. It would appear that by the end of the 15th century these tribes had moved as far as present-day Zambia, Rhodesia and Mozambique. They probably crossed into the present-day Republic of South Africa in appreciable numbers in the course of the 17th century—at about the same time as the Afrikaner freefarmers' settlement was expanding inland from the Cape of Good Hope.[2]

Politicians' speeches are apt to refer to the myth of simultaneous migrations. Some do so in almost exactly the same words as the Department of Information in its annual publication. Thus on 24 October 1974 R. F. (Pik) Botha, South African Foreign Minister, declared to the United Nations Security Council: 'About the middle of the seventeenth century, the white and black peoples of southern Africa converged upon what was then an almost uninhabited part of the continent.'

A year later Louis Pienaar, the South African ambassador in Paris, wrote in the *Revue des Deux Mondes*: 'The black peoples of South Africa, who came from countries further to the north, emigrated to what is now the Republic of South Africa at roughly the time when the Europeans were settling in the south of the continent.'[3]

Other politicians do not hesitate to amplify the historical falsification, and even go so far as to declare that the whites came first. Thus C. P. Mulder told the World Affairs Council at Los Angeles on 6 June 1975: 'The Bantu were not indigenous. They came after the Dutch and the British.'[4]

Unlike politicians, who repeat or amplify the official doctrine, recent school textbooks put it more subtly. In a Standard-8 textbook published in 1974, for instance, we read: 'Southern Africa is not the original home of the southern Bantu, who are immigrants as are the whites. . . . It is not known precisely when the vanguard of the movement reached South Africa, but there is evidence that it was in, or just before, the fifteenth century.'[5]

This 'just before' also appeared in July 1975 in the

1. *South Africa 77*, p. 82.
2. *Multi-national Development in South Africa, the Reality*, State Department of Information, Pretoria, 1974, p. 22.
3. *Revue des Deux Mondes*, December 1975.
4. *The Unesco Courier*, November 1977, p. 10.
5. *Senior Secondary History for Standard Eight*, p. 102.

explanatory notes on the ethnological display cases in the Cape Museum: 'Traditions put the earliest arrivals at some time before the sixteenth century, but Iron Age settlements north of the Orange River, with dwellings like those of the historic Tswana, have been dated somewhat earlier.'[1]

Foreign versions of the myth

The vast majority of books about South Africa by non-South Africans make history begin with Bartholomew Diaz's discovery of the Cape of Good Hope in 1488, and only mention the blacks from the time of their meeting with the whites in about 1778. This is hardly surprising, since these books are based on official documentation that ignores the pre-European history of the blacks.

Unfortunately some historians who claim to specialize in black Africa have recently written about South Africa without taking into account the proof that the blacks came first, as detailed articles have established since the beginning of the 1960s. In 1969, these articles were made available to the general public in Volume I of the *Oxford History of South Africa*, edited by two world-famous South African historians, Monica Wilson and Leonard Thompson. Two of these 'specialists' will be quoted later, since their work has been widely disseminated throughout Africa, either in the original English editions (1962 and 1969) or in the translations distributed at an exceptionally low price in French-speaking Africa (1962 and 1977).

Refutation: the Early Iron Age in South Africa, third century to the eleventh

Archaeological research carried out in the provinces of the Transvaal, Natal and the Orange Free State had by 1978 yielded a more precise picture of ancient settlements than the one presented by Monica Wilson in 1969. The interested reader will find a separate section in the bibliography listing the main articles published on this subject since 1970 in various scientific journals. We shall confine ourselves to giving a broad outline of what is known about the history of the blacks before the eleventh century.

Outside South Africa, the great majority of historians nowadays agree that it was Bantu-speaking blacks who introduced iron metallurgy south of the equator.

Thus the term 'Bantu' covers two cultural features: (a) the

1. Display case dealing with the Sotho.

use of a language fairly close but certainly related to a primal Bantu language, which probably originated in the Benue River area in middle Nigeria, and (b) knowledge of iron metallurgy.

By contrast, the term 'Bantu' has no precise meaning in terms of physical anthropology, since in the course of their southward migration the Bantu-speaking peoples mixed to a varying extent with Khoisan-type populations, who had peopled southern Africa since an unknown date.

In other words, while there is the idea of a Bantu language (introduced in 1862 by the German linguist Bleek) and also that of a Bantu civilization, it is totally incorrect to speak of a Bantu 'race'. Hence it is particularly shocking to read in an American book published in 1970:

A full-scale Iron Age culture was established between the Zambesi and the Limpopo by the end of the fourth century. There is no assurance that all this was the work of early Bantu settlers; however the most plausible alternative is that these Iron Age sites resulted from adaptation of an infiltrating Bantu economy and culture by resident Bushmen or Hottentots with the prospect of Bantu settlers soon to follow.[1]

World history offers no example of a people adopting an alien culture away from the physical presence of the owners of that culture. It is deplorable that the writer of the last sentence should not have admitted (as historical research has amply demonstrated) that Iron Age civilization was introduced into South Africa by Bantu-speaking blacks.

The first millennium is the period known as the Early Iron Age, when small groups of blacks settled in the Transvaal and northern Natal and gradually mixed with the Khoisan-type population.

The earliest Iron Age site to have been discovered is in the Zoutpansberg Mountains (northern Transvaal). Dated to the third century A.D. (H. P. Prinsloo, 1974), it yielded a type of pottery related to the Gokomere type often met in Zimbabwe (Rhodesia).

For climatic and ecological reasons archaeologists have taken a particular interest in the so-called Lowveld area that covers eastern Transvaal and Swaziland. Lying between the cold, inhospitable Drakensberg Range and the Lebombo Range (which roughly marks the border of the Transvaal and Swaziland with Mozambique), the Lowveld is a strip approximately 100 kilometres wide, a good half of which is now occupied by the Kruger National Park.

There is good reason to believe that in the first millennium

1. Robert W. July, *A History of the African People*, New York, 1970, p. 134.

this north–south corridor acted as a dispersal centre for groups who later made their way either to the plateau west of the Drakensberg (the Transvaal Sotho) or to the east towards the more low-lying areas of Mozambique and Natal (the Nguni). This at any rate seems to be the inference from the datings, ranging from the fourth to the ninth century, of several dozens of early Iron Age sites in north-east Transvaal, Swaziland and northern Natal (M. Klapwijk, 1973 and 1974; T. M. Evers, 1975; T. P. Dutton, 1970). In the southern Transvaal, several sites on the outskirts of Pretoria have also been dated to the fifth and sixth centuries. Some of them contain Negro-type skeletons and a richly decorated pottery (R. J. Mason, 1973, 1974). Up to the time of writing (1978) no early Iron Age sites have been discovered in the Orange Free State, Natal south of the latitude of Durban, or the Cape Province. These areas were presumably peopled exclusively by Khoisan during the first millennium.

On the other hand, it is fair to say that the ancestors of the South African blacks were established south of the Limpopo in the third century, and not 'in the sixteenth century or slightly earlier' as the official history claims. It would also be fair to say that during the first millennium there were sedentary settlements of miners and farmers. Traces of millet cultivation (*Pennisetum americanum*) have been found at the Silver Leaves site dated to the third century, and several permanent settlements of iron smelters and salt panners have been dated to the fourth and fifth centuries. These discoveries, and, *a fortiori*, those that relate to the period from the eleventh century to the eighteenth, flatly contradict a second myth in South African history that is a corollary to the first. It will be considered in the next chapter.

7 Myth II

*That the blacks were migrants
until they met the whites*

Versions of the myth

As given by South Africans

South Africa 1977 devotes only a few lines to the question:

It was not before 1770, at the Great Fish River, that the Afrikaner stock-farmer encountered the vanguard of the black or Bantu peoples who, during the course of centuries, had been migrating slowly southwards on a broad transcontinental front. Those on the Fish River were the Xhosa, the spearhead of other tribes of the Nguni group who were later to form the Zulu and Swazi nations.[1]

The Nguni linguistic group is by far the largest in South Africa (10 million Nguni-speakers in 1976), and lives all along the east coast from the Mozambique border (Zulu and Swazi) to the Transkei and the Ciskei (Xhosa). To quote from a Standard-8 textbook published in 1974:

The name Nguni is a collective name for several hundred tribes, who are thought to have spread into southern Africa in the fifteenth century. Crossing the Limpopo, they reached the central Transvaal, where certain tribes, especially the Ndebele, remained. However, most of the tribes crossed the Drakensberg where, in the course of time, they settled in the land between the mountains and the sea from Swaziland through Natal down to the eastern Cape. Here they divided into different groups—the Swazi in Swaziland, the Zulu in northern Natal and the Xhosa in the Transkei. *The south-western migration of the Nguni was checked in 1770 at the Fish River*, where it clashed with the north-eastern migration of the cattle-farmers.[2]

. *South Africa 1977*, p. 40.
. *Senior Secondary History or Standard Eight*, 1974, . 102.

The Sotho linguistic group lives mainly in the Transvaal and the Orange Free State. This is what another Standard-8 history book, published in 1975, says about it:

The Sotho people came from the Great Lake area in Central Africa. It is accepted that their migration to the south also took about 2,000 years. *They occupied the central parts of southern Africa south of the Zambesi and north of the Orange River in three groups, between the years 1300 and 1400. Some authorities are of the opinion that they only reached their present territories in the year 1600.*[1]

The italicized sentences (our emphasis) in the two previous quotations sum up the historical falsification that we shall refute in the second part of this chapter.

As embroidered by foreigners

It must be said that these official South African textbooks of 1974 and 1975 are relatively moderate in comparison with the account given by the South African historian E. A. Walker in *A History of South Africa*, published in 1928, which for the third edition in 1957 became *A History of Southern Africa*. In the 1962 edition the author says (without emphasizing the point) that the South African Nguni originated in whole or in part from the southward migration of the fierce Abambo and Amazimba, who according to Portuguese sources had pillaged the coast of what is now Kenya at the end of the sixteenth century:

There came waves of Bantu invaders from the north, the Abambo and the Amazimba, fierce men, cannibals on occasion and at all times slaughterers of the peaceful Makaranga . . .[2]

The survivors of the Makaranga had remained in Portuguese East Africa after the ferocious Abambo and Amazimba had swept away southwards . . .[3]

These coast tribes [the Nguni] had arisen out of the chaos produced by the incursion of the Abambo and Amazimba into what are now Zululand and Natal. Early in the seventeenth century, either those invaders or the wrecks of the tribes they had driven before them or all of them had broken up in the neighbourhood of the Tugela river and formed new tribes . . . the bulk of them either stayed where they were or pushed slowly down the coast belt towards the Colony. The Xhosas came first . . .[4]

It is most regrettable that this theory—nonsense for any historian worthy of the name—should have been uncritically reproduced and even simplified by the American D. L. Wiedner:

1. *History and Geography* Standard Eight, 1975, p. 63
2. Eric A. Walker, *A History of Southern Africa*, 1962, p. 20.
3. Ibid., p. 109.
4. Ibid., p. 110.

After the Sotho and Ngoni marauders had ravaged the Monomotapa lands and disrupted Portuguese Mozambique between 1590
and 1620, they crossed the Limpopo River into South Africa. . . .
The Ngoni, who were the earlier and fiercer invaders, took the
semitropical coastlands of modern Natal for themselves. As they
came over the Drakensberg Mountains from the Transvaal, they
split into four groups to occupy the new country: Swazi the
northeast, then Zulu, Pondo, Tembu and Xhosa along the coast
toward the Cape. When they reached the Kei River about 1700,
their conquering urge was, for the time, satisfied. . . . The Sotho
remained in the interior, between the Drakensberg and the
Kalahari. The southern branch arrived during the seventeenth
century in the modern Orange Free State; the northern Sotho
remained in the Transvaal.[1]

On page 116 of Wiedner's book a map subtitled 'The
Occupation of South Africa before 1652' illustrates the
foregoing account with three black arrows: the westernmost
arrow, marked 'Sotho', crosses the Zambezi in 1620 and
arrives north of the Limpopo in 1650; the middle arrow,
marked 'Ngoni', crosses the Zambezi in 1590 and the
Limpopo in 1620, and stops in 1650 not in the coastal area
where the peoples of the Nguni group live but right in the
middle of the Transvaal; a third arrow, marked 'Rozwi',
crosses the Zambezi 'in the fourteenth century' and stops
at Zimbabwe 'in the fourteenth–fifteenth century'.
　　Thus this book, which appeared in 1962 and has been
very widely disseminated, especially in French-speaking
Africa, uncritically reproduces the interpretations put forward
at the very beginning of the century by the great South
African historian G. McCall Theal (1837–1919)[2] and repeated
by E. A. Walker, namely that the ancestors of the Nguni (not
Ngoni, as Wiedner spells it) were the Mumbo mentioned
by the Dominican João dos Santos in his *Ethiopia Oriental*
published at Evora, Portugal, in 1609. The Mumbo (or
Abambo) were the neighbours of the notorious Muzimba (or
Amazimba) cannibals who in about 1590 launched a destructive raid on the coast of modern Kenya as far as Malindi,
where João dos Santos abandons them to their sad fate without
a word about the southward migration described by Walker
and Wiedner. Monomotapa was indeed destroyed by the
Nguni (Ndebele and Ngoni), but only in 1830 and by an
invasion from the south and not the north.
　　Apart from the geographical statements about the present-
day whereabouts of the various Nguni and Sotho groups,
the passage quoted is untrue from beginning to end.

1. D. L. Wiedner, *A History
of Africa South of the Sahara*,
New York, 1962, p. 115.
2. G. McCall Theal, *Records
of South Eastern Africa*,
9 Vols., Cape Town,
1898–1903.

Refutation: history of South African blacks from the eleventh century to the eighteenth

The diversity of the sources

For geographical reasons, the documentation sources are very different for the two major linguistic groups in South Africa.

The Sotho live west of the Drakensberg Range on the 'central plateau' (altitude between 1,200 and 1,800 metres), which covers the Transvaal, the Orange Free State and the north-eastern Cape Province. The nature of the soil and subsoil is such that stone buildings and old mine-workings are extremely widespread. The Transvaal in particular represents the favoured terrain for South African archaeology, which has yielded very valuable information about the ancestors of the modern Sotho (Northern Sotho or Pedi, Southern Sotho or Shweshwe and Western Sotho or Tswana) and of the Shona, the predecessors of the modern Venda (half a million in 1976) who live in the very north of the Transvaal.

The coastal area east of the Drakensberg range that covers Natal, the Transkei and the Ciskei is occupied by the Nguni all the way from Mozambique to Port Elizabeth. This is the best watered area in the whole of South Africa; it is particularly good for agriculture and cattle-raising, but it lacks mineral resources. Stone buildings are virtually non-existent. Hence archaeology has yielded very little data. But several accounts by shipwreck survivors establish the presence of Nguni-speaking peoples in the north of the modern Transkei in the middle of the sixteenth century (100 years before the whites arrived at the Cape).

The small group of the Tsonga or Shangaan (800,000 in 1976), which is the fourth linguistic group in South Africa, came from Mozambique, and the historical sources are similar to those of the Nguni (Zulu, Xhosa, Swazi and Ndebele).

The Sotho-Tswana linguistic group
(Tswana, Southern Sotho and Northern Sotho)

Archaeology has thrown considerable light on the early history of the Sotho by demonstrating the existence of close cultural affinities between some sedentary communities of cultivators, cattle-breeders and miners settled in South Africa since the eleventh century and the various communities today associated with the Sotho-Tswana group.

The true homeland of the Sotho-Tswana, i.e. their original

population centre, is in the west and centre of the southern Transvaal, more precisely in a semi-circular area probably centred on Pretoria and the Magaliesberg range and extending as far as Zeerust in the west, the Vaal River in the South and Lydenberg (250 kilometres from Pretoria) in the north-east.[1]

The extraordinary density of the ancient iron and tin mines, and still more of the ancient stone buildings, has long impressed observers, and led the South African prehistorian R. J. Mason to say that the population figure in this area might have reached several hundred thousand in about the sixteenth century. The rapid growth in population was certainly fostered by the excellent climate and fine grazing, and also by the large mineral resources. To judge by the profusion of beads found at the sites of mining operations, the trade in metals (tin, copper, salt and especially iron) must have been substantial. But it seems to have remained local; no other imported objects have been found.

We have very few datings, but there are many indications that between the eleventh and fifteenth centuries population movements were also localized within the central area. There were very many small-scale movements, and not 'three great migratory waves from north of the Limpopo between 1300 and 1400' as the official history states. The slowness of the process accounts for the excellent integration into black society of the Khoisan-type natives who lived in these areas before the coming—in the fifth century at least—of the very first Early Iron Age groups. It must have been these Khoisan who taught the blacks stock-breeding techniques, since the Sotho vocabulary pertaining to livestock is Khoisan and not Bantu.

As early as the fifteenth century the ancestors of the present-day Southern Sotho, outgrowing the population centre, crossed the Vaal and settled in the fertile lands in the north-east of the modern Orange Free State (T. Maggs, 1973); and oral tradition places the migration of the Bafokeng from Magaliesberg to the fertile valley of the lower Caledon in about 1500.

Before going further, it may be necessary to point out that the expansion of the Sotho-Tswana people between the eleventh and sixteenth centuries occurred in a specially favoured area of South Africa (from the point of view of agriculture and mining), and that the whole of this area today belongs to the 'white homeland'. The poor-quality lands regarded—wrongly—as the 'historic homelands' of the Sotho-Tswana, namely Bophuthatswana and Botswana,

1. See Map 2, p. 16.

Lesotho and Lebowa (Northern Sotho), were only settled in a later 'expansion' phase that succeeded the initial 'settlement' phase.

The expansion phase which began in the fifteenth century continued in the seventeenth and eighteenth. By the end of the eighteenth century the expansion area of the Sotho peoples extended in four main directions:[1] to the north-east the Northern Sotho had reached the Limpopo in the Messina area and mixed extensively with other black tribes from north of the Limpopo; to the north the Tswana (Western Sotho) were established beyond the upper reaches of the Limpopo in the south of present-day Botswana as far as the Gaborone area; to the west other Tswana, intermingled with the native Khoisan populations, occupied in large numbers the extreme north-east of the modern Cape Province, known between 1884 and 1895 as British Bechuanaland (Chuana = Tswana); and to the south the Southern Sotho, descended directly from Tswana clans and also intermixed with Khoisan, occupied the modern Orange Free State except for its western third—in modern Lesotho they only occupied the western fringe.

The area of distribution of the Sotho at the end of the eighteenth century calls for several comments. First, it was approximately five times greater in extent than the total area allocated by Pretoria to the three Sotho homelands (Lebowa, Bophuthatswana and Qwaqwa). Secondly, as regards rainfall: apart from the former British Bechuanaland, which has between 300 and 500 mm of rain a year and can only support a pastoral economy, the Sotho settled east of the 600-mm isohyet, which demarcates the limits of non-irrigated agriculture. In what is now Botswana and Lesotho they occupied only the very narrow strip of arable land amounting to approximately 5 per cent of the area of each of these countries. The migrations of the various groups were therefore checked not by the whites, as the official history claims, but by climatic and ecological factors. This is even clearer in the case of the Nguni migrations, as we shall see.

Of the three major Sotho groups only the Tswana (Western Sotho) had contact with whites before the time of the Great Trek.

The visitors of the first two decades of the nineteenth century, travellers or missionaries, were all impressed by the size of the Tswana towns, surrounded by circular stone walls, and by the order that seemed to prevail in them. They noted with admiration the level of agriculture, the size of

1. See Map 3, p. 17.

the herds, the skill of the craftsmen and the brisk trade in hides, skins and various iron and copper articles.

In the former British Bechuanaland the town of Kithakong, often known as Littakao, had a population of about 15,000 in 1801 divided into fifty or so sections, each under the authority of a chief. This administrative system seems to have facilitated the absorption of foreign groups within a political entity: some sections consisted entirely of foreigners, who kept their own chiefs.

In the western Transvaal the town of Kaditshwena, capital of the Hurutshe Tswana, when visited in 1815 by the missionary J. Campbell, apparently had the same number of inhabitants as Dithakong and the same system of division into sections.

These descriptions of black societies at the end of the eighteenth century, civilized, orderly and relatively prosperous, thanks to a lively trade, never appear in school textbooks, and still less in the official literature intended for foreigners.

The Venda and their Shona predecessors:
the Mapungubwe treasures

The main archaeological site in South Africa is associated not with the Sotho but with the Shona from beyond the Limpopo, who preceded the Venda in the extreme north of the Transvaal.

The sacred hill of Mapungubwe is on the Transvaal bank of the Limpopo, in an area that is deserted today because of its unhealthy climate. The hill rises steeply on all sides and, for the few inhabitants of the area, was a place forbidden by the ancestors. It was only with great difficulty that the Boer farmer Van Graaf in 1933 found a guide willing to show him the way to the top. After an arduous ascent through a passage hollowed out of the cliff, Van Graaf and his companions were amazed to discover, on the relatively small flat area on the top of the hill, first beads and bits of copper and iron, and then numerous gold objects, beads, bracelets and rhinoceros-shaped plaques over two kilograms altogether. Lastly, they discovered the remains of a skeleton, which unfortunately crumbled to dust on exposure to the air.

These were the first gold artefacts ever found in South Africa; and the archaeological committee of the University of Pretoria, realizing the importance of this discovery by 'amateurs', organized a campaign of officially supervised excavations in 1934–35. These were rewarded at the outset

by the discovery of another two kilograms of gold in the
form of beads and chased plaques and, above all, a 'royal
burial ground' containing the fragments of thirty-three
skeletons.

In 1937 Leo Fouché, a professor at the University of
Pretoria, published the results with nine co-workers in a
lavishly illustrated 200-page large-format volume brought out
in Cambridge. The title of the book, *Mapungubwe—An
Ancient Bantu Civilization on the Limpopo*, summarized the
conclusions reached by the archaeologists.

Obviously they believed that this was a 'purely Bantu
civilization'. N. Jones and J. F. Schofield, who were in charge
of the 1934–35 excavations, stressed the similarities to that
of the builders of Zimbabwe; and Fouché in the final chapter
stated that the links between the Shona of the Matopo
mountains (south of Bulawayo) and the inhabitants of the
Mapungubwe area were not only commercial but also
religious. He wrote:

Fifty years ago, the Mwari priests levied tribute from chiefs,
great and small, all over the Zoutpansberg district in the Transvaal.
These chiefs sent their trusted messengers with gifts of ivory and
black beasts to propitiate the god in his holy of holies, a cave in
the Matopos. . . . Some say that tribute is still so paid to-day.[1]

Even though he took pains to have his book published in
England, the fact remains that Leo Fouché was a white South
African of Afrikaner stock. In asserting the black origin of an
ancient and highly developed civilization he was openly
opposing the historical Afrikaner creed that 'the blacks who
arrived in the seventeenth century led a wild nomadic life
until the time when they met the whites'.

Given these heretical statements by the archaeologists,
the Pretoria authorities defended themselves cleverly by
calling upon the anthropologist A. Galloway to study the
skeletons discovered in the royal burial ground. Galloway's
conclusions, which occupy a quarter of the book, fitted the
historical creed admirably. He asserted that the eleven skeletons analysed were all of the Bush-Boskopoid type (i.e. pre-
Hottentot), 'with some rare Negroid traits'. He even went
as far as to make an unexpected value judgement, stating
that 'the absence of Negro impurity in the Sceptre skeleton,
presumably that of a leader among his people, whose blood
would unlikely be defiled by the arrival of a sporadic alien,
is particularly striking'.[2]

Despite the reassuring nature of the anthropologist's
words, it was thought preferable to 'bury' the heresies put

1. L. Fouché, *Mapungubwe*,
p. 177.
2. A. Galloway, 'The Skeletal
Remains of Mapungubwe',
p. 127–76, in *Mapungubwe*,
1937.

forward by the archaeologists. Instead of the dozen experts requested by Leo Fouché to continue the excavations, only one was appointed, namely Captain G. A. Gardner, who actively devoted himself to the task between 1935 and 1940, but had to wait fifteen years before publishing three brief articles in the *South African Archaeological Bulletin*, first in 1955 and then in 1958 and 1959. It was not until 1963, a year after the author's death, that Gardner's book *Mapungubwe, Vol. II* about the overall findings of the 1935–40 excavations was published in Pretoria.

Meanwhile two carbon-14 datings to the fourteenth and the fifteenth century had been obtained for the Mapungubwe site, and Galloway had published a paper in 1959 on forty of the seventy-four skeletons discovered in 1937 by Gardner at the Bambandyanalo site near Mapungubwe, which has been dated to the eleventh century. In this paper Galloway stated 'deliberately and with full comprehension of its significance that there is not a single specifically Negro feature in any skull hitherto recovered at Bambandyanalo'.[1]

In *Mapungubwe II* Gardner upheld Galloway's anthropological conclusions. He systematically emphasized the pastoral features of the civilization of the occupants of the Bambandyanalo site, while equally systematically disregarding its agricultural features in order to establish its 'Hottentot' rather than 'Negro' origin. By so doing he made an appreciable 'scientific' contribution to the ideology of apartheid. While Afrikaners think it dangerous to attribute to the blacks a developed pre-European civilization such as Mapungubwe, they see no difficulty in assigning a brilliant past to the Hottentots and Bushmen, whose forebears peopled the whole of southern Africa, but whose few modern representatives lead a deplorably limited life.

However, during the abnormally long interval that elapsed between the end of Gardner's excavations (1940) and the publication of his book (1963), improved archaeological techniques had led to an entirely new theory of the Bantu migrations north of the Limpopo during the first millennium. The denial of a black presence south of the Limpopo before the seventeenth century consequently struck the specialists who read *Mapungubwe II* as highly suspect.

In 1964 the prehistorian Brian Fagan, a specialist in Zambian archaeology, at last brought some clarity to the confused argument about the Hottentot or Negro origin of the Mapungubwe treasures. In an article in the *Journal of African History*,[2] he established on irrefutable grounds; first, that the bearers of the Iron Age culture had crossed

1. A. Galloway, *The Skeletal Remains of Bamdandyanalo*, Johannesburg, 1959.
2. Brian Fagan, 'The Greefswald Sequence: Bambandyanalo and Mapungubwe', *Journal of African History*, Vol. 3, 1964, p. 337–61.

the Limpopo during the first millennium; second, that the occupants of Bambandyanalo at the beginning of the eleventh century were culturally very close to the makers of the so-called Gokomere pottery settled on the Rhodesian plateau; third, that the occupants of Mapungubwe between 1100 and 1500 were very probably Shona, but that their small number accounted for the long persistence of the Khoisan physical type, which formed the large majority for several centuries; and fourth that the Venda arrived after the Shona had left the sacred hill of Mapungubwe in about 1500.

The number and quality of the objects found at Mapungubwe suggest that there was brisk trading activity in the fourteenth and fifteenth centuries in the Limpopo valley and along its northern tributaries that come down from the Rhodesian plateau. The copper no doubt came from the nearby Messina mines, which are known to have been worked at the time, and the iron was extracted in the Zoutpansberg mountains one hundred or so kilometres to the south. The gold came from further afield, probably from Olifant's River or the Barberton area in north-eastern Transvaal.

Apart from these materials of African origin, the Mapungubwe finds included beads and porcelain from China and also clothing, probably imported through Delagoa Bay (south of the mouth of the Limpopo), where a Portuguese ship is known to have called every year in the second half of the sixteenth century to buy copper and ivory.

The Tsonga and the Delagoa Bay trade

In the seventeenth and eighteenth centuries Delagoa Bay (Mozambique), a port of call for British, Indian, Dutch and French ships, witnessed a considerable expansion of trade as a result of the activities of the Tsonga (today settled mainly in Mozambique, with smaller settlements in Gazankulu in the north-eastern Transvaal), who had organized a complex trading network throughout the Transvaal in conjunction with the Venda, Phalaborwa and Pedi (Northern Sotho).

This remarkable trading activity on the part of the Tsonga, the Venda (A. Smith, 1970) and the Pedi (M. Legassik, 1969) is never mentioned in South African history books.

The Xhosa up to the end of the eighteenth century

The Xhosa or Cape Nguni, the southernmost branch of the Nguni linguistic group, settled in the Transkei and the Ciskei, feature prominently in the myth of 'black migrations pursued until they met the whites'.

During the seventy years that elapsed between the first significant clash between blacks and whites in 1770 (an earlier encounter between small groups of hunters had taken place in 1702) and the beginning of the Great Trek, the Xhosa were the only blacks of whom the whites had direct knowledge. Consequently they were for a long time identified with the whole South African black population, as witness the phrase 'Kaffir Wars' or 'Xhosa Wars', applied indiscriminately to the nine frontier conflicts between blacks and whites in the troubled Fish River area between 1779 and 1879. The word *kaffir* (from an Arabic word meaning 'infidel') was for a long time used to designate all South African blacks.

This being so, it is hardly surprising that in the official history of South Africa the usual clichés are applied to the Xhosa. They are supposed to have arrived in what is now Transkei after the whites arrived at the Cape; and their migration is supposed to have been comparable to the barbarian invasions in Europe after the decline of the Roman Empire.

As early as 1959 Monica Wilson[1] had revealed the falsity of these assertions and recent multidisciplinary research has confirmed her hypotheses.[2]

Admittedly the archaeological poverty of the area makes dating extremely difficult. But for the period 1552–1645 we have six accounts by survivors from Portuguese ships wrecked on the east coast. Critical new studies of these documents have led to a modification of the fanciful conclusions reached by Theal and repeated by Walker and Wiedner. The report by the survivors of the *Santo Alberto*, wrecked in 1593, gives a detailed description of a long journey into the interior of what is now the Transkei and notes the existence of sedentary settlements of Xhosa blacks separated by enormous uninhabited areas, including the slopes of the Drakensberg, which were frequented by San hunters (Bushmen) and what is now the Ciskei, where Khoi (Hottentot) cattle-breeders had lived since the eleventh century.

The reports by the survivors of the *São João Baptista* (1622), the *Nossa Senhora de Belem* (1635) and the *Sacramento* (1645) make it clear that Xhosa blacks had already crossed the Kei River (the border between the Transkei and the Ciskei) before the whites settled at the Cape.

To turn to the Xhosa migrations, it is certain that they

1. M. Wilson, 'The Early History of the Transkei and Ciskei', *African Studies*, Vol. 4, 1959, p. 167–79.
2. R. M. Devricourt (ed.), *Prehistoric Man in the Ciskei and Transkei*, Cape Town, 1977.

went on throughout the eighteenth century. But, contrary
to the view long put forward in the official history, they
never took the form of massive population movements,
and, more important, were not stopped by the whites in 1770,
but by climatic and ecological factors. The importance of
the latter may be gauged by relating the areas of Xhosa
settlement in the eighteenth century to the 600 mm isohyet,
which determines the possibility of non-irrigated agriculture
and of cattle-breeding (see Figs. 3 and 4, p. 17–18).

From the very beginning of the eighteenth century small
groups of Xhosa cattle-breeders had established themselves
in mountainous, well-watered expanses of land in the area
west of the 600 mm isohyet. Thus the very first encounter
between whites and Xhosa blacks in 1702 took place near
present-day Somerset East, in the damp area of Bruintjes
Hoogte, where the border of the Dutch Cape Colony was
to be fixed in 1770. At that time the nucleus of Xhosa settlement was east of the Fish River (which forms the southern
border of the Ciskei), but some Xhosa families had emigrated
to try to find good grazing in the Zuurveld (the present-day
Grahamstown area), and had mixed with the Khoi groups
(Hottentot) already there. The long peaceful cohabitation
of Khoi and Xhosa is attested by the frequency of very
light skin among the Xhosa and by the 2,500 words containing
clicks found in the Xhosa language, compared with only 375
in Zulu (despite the fact that 80 per cent of the roots are
common to both languages).

In 1778, when they pushed the frontier of the Colony
back to the Fish River, the whites thus took possession of
a territory traversed and inhabited by increasing numbers of
Xhosa, who there came to the end of the area climatically
suitable for cattle-breeding. But for the whites, after 700 kilometres of dryness, this area initially looked like a promised
land. Hence the troubled history of the area, where nine
'Kaffir Wars' were to take place between 1779 and 1878.

8 Myth III

That Chaka, Dingaan and Mzilikazi were nothing but bloodthirsty despots

The refutation of this myth is to be found in Zulu history from 1795 to 1837.

Chaka[1]

From *South Africa 1977*: 'Chaka's rule completely changed the demographic structure of Natal between 1815 and 1825. One tribe after another was attacked and destroyed, usually after their chiefs and headmen had been murdered. . . . By 1826 only thirty-three tribes or half of the former population were left.'[2] The same volume also says:

Chaka was responsible for a reign of terror unparalleled in those times. In the process he converted the erstwhile weak Zulu into a nation whose reputation for military prowess was to penetrate far beyond the borders of South Africa. His top warriors practised celibacy before campaigns. Combining the short stabbing assegai with the crescent formation of attack, they became the scourge of the south-eastern continents.[3]

These passages on Chaka are marked by both fabrication and omission. Regarding the statement that 'by 1826 only thirty-three tribes or half of the former population were left' in Natal, one wonders where these figures came from. Nathaniel Isaacs's 'diary' contains the following lines:

In 1828 it is quite clear, also, that the people must be numerous from the thickly settled hamlets which the face of the whole country exhibits; and those hamlets appear to contain, each of them, a great many persons of all ages. Within a short period,

1. The name is frequently spelled 'Shaka'.
2. *South Africa 1977*, p. 85, 86.
3. Ibid., p. 82.

our settlement at Port Natal [present-day Durban], which was somewhat circumscribed, contained upwards of two thousand persons.[1]

Shula Marks, who quotes this passage in her paper 'Shaka Zulu', published in 1977 in Volume II of *Les Africains*, adds that 'the traditions of the day also spoke of numerous chiefdoms which were practically adjoining'.

Nathaniel Isaacs, who came to Port Natal in 1825 as a young trader, is one of the only two writers who knew Chaka personally and left eyewitness accounts of Natal before the death of the great Zulu king. This being so, it is hard to see why it was necessary to reject as invalid the passage quoted and to accept the figures provided by the missionary A. T. Bryant, who arrived in Natal sixty years later.

Falsification by omission is hardly unique to South African historians, but in the specific case of Chaka it must be recognized that the official version given above completely prevents the reader from appreciating the historical import- ance of this exceptional African for not only south-east Africa but for the whole of the black continent.

The novelty and originality of the fighting methods adopted by the king of the Zulus are indeed mentioned, but apparently only to emphasize their role both quantitative and qualitative in the extension of terror.

Nothing is said about the new organization of the army, which had far-reaching sociological effects. Chaka's genius lay in setting up a military state in which territorial commands were given not to members of the royal family, but to *indunas*, military chiefs from either his own clan or a subject tribe whom he appointed and dismissed. This system made pos- sible the remarkably rapid and stable integration of the subject tribes into the emergent Zulu nation.

Between 1815 and 1822, the chief of a small tribe from northern Natal accomplished the absolute *tour de force* of implanting the Zulu language and culture throughout Natal and as far as Malawi and Tanzania, 1,500 miles away, where Zulu-speaking Ngoni still live, descendents of the small groups brought there by Chaka's dissident generals.

There are few comparable examples of integration in world history. But this the official history does not mention.

1. N. Isaacs, *Travels and Adventures in Eastern Africa* Vol. II, p. 269.

Dingaan

South Africa 1977 makes only a passing reference to Chaka's successor on the Zulu throne:

Trekking in groups across vast tracts that had been depopulated by war among the black races themselves before the advent of the whites, the Voortrekkers soon had to fight for their lives against two black despots. The first was Mzilikazi, a refugee Zulu general who with his Matabele tribe dominated the high plateau, the second, Dingaan, king of the Zulu, who ruled Natal from his seat north of the Tugela River.[1]

By contrast, a Standard-6 textbook devotes three and a half pages to Dingaan in a twenty-page chapter (chapter 10) entitled 'the Great Trek'. Dingaan's personality also is dealt with in the sections on Piet Retief (six pages) and Andries Pretorius (six pages). Whereas the latter two are sympathetically presented, the description of Dingaan stresses only his negative aspects:

Dingaan, born about 1795 . . . murdered his half-brother Chaka in 1828 and took his place as King of the Zulu. Being large and corpulent (fat) he was inclined to be indolent (lazy). The name given to his kraal, Ungungundhlovu (the place of the great elephant) expresses his opinion of his greatness. Like most primitive people, he was blood-thirsty and seemed to exult when his enemies were beaten to death. . . . Any offence even on the part of a relative was punished with death.[2]

Having thus described Dingaan's laziness and in particular his cruelty, the textbook gives a condescending account of the naivety and supposed gullibility of the Zulu king: 'Dingaan's first sight of Retief (in November 1837) had puzzled him. He had once before met a man called Piet (Piet Uys on his 'Commissie Trek') who had spoken to him about land and now Piet (Piet Retief) was back again but he looked entirely different. The man must be a wizard.'[3]

Next comes a summary of the reasons that supposedly prompted Dingaan to order the massacre of Piet Retief and his party of sixty-six men, four boys and thirty coloured servants on 6 February 1838. As details of the slaughter are given in the previous section on Piet Retief, the textbook confines itself to an overall assessment: 'We have already learnt how cunningly Dingaan planned Retief's murder and with what cruelty it was carried out.'[4]

In February, April and August 1838, the Zulu again inflicted heavy losses on the 4,000 Voortrekkers who hoped

South Africa 1977, p. 42.
Junior Secondary History
r Standard Six, 1974, p. 144.
Ibid., p. 144.
Ibid., p. 145.

to establish themselves in Natal: they lost about 300 of their number and as many coloured servants, along with a great deal of livestock.

Then on 16 December 1838 Dingaan's army was routed at the famous battle of Blood River; 3,000 Zulu perished at a cost of three white casualties. Dingaan himself, defeated in January 1840 by his half-brother Mpande, who had rallied to the Voortrekkers, fled to what is now Swaziland, where he was assassinated by a Swazi.

Having narrated these events, which took place after the murder of Piet Retief, the chapter ends with an expression of astonishment that reveals the Afrikaner mentality: 'Although he [Dingaan] died in ignominy his people did not forget him and he ranks with the great kings of the Zulu, Chaka [died 1828], Cetshwayo [1884] and Dinizulu [1913], in Zulu history.'[1]

Throughout their school years, white South Africans have learnt to hate and despise the two 'black despots', Mzikilazi and Dingaan, who dared to oppose the Voortrekkers' advance into the Transvaal and Natal. It would therefore seem abnormal to them that anyone should revere their memory. But a critical examination of the primary sources for their period produces a much more subtle image of these two figures and provides a firm foundation for the admiration shown for them by Africans.

Only four writers were directly acquainted with Dingaan: two young traders by the names of Henry Francis Fynn[2] and Nathaniel Isaacs[3] who arrived at Port Natal in 1824 and 1825, and two American missionaries working for the Anglican mission, Allen P. Gardiner[4] and F. Owen,[5] who arrived in 1835 and 1837. All writings about Dingaan draw on one or another of these sources, often exaggerating the others' accounts.

A critical study of these four writers which appeared in the *Journal of African History*[6] in 1969 demonstrates the way European traders at Port Natal repeatedly broke their word and continually infringed the provisions of a treaty concluded in May 1835. The treaty, drafted by Gardiner, asked Europeans not to give asylum to fugitives from the Zulu kingdom, and asked Dingaan not to attack property or persons settled at Port Natal. In 1837 the whites officially repudiated the treaty and halted the sale of gunpowder. For his part, Piet Retief, who had pledged to give Dingaan sixty-three horses and eleven rifles captured from Chief Sikonyela, delivered only the animals.

Dingaan's 'treachery and cunning' were in a way his

1. *Junior Secondary Histor* *for Standard Six*, 1974, p. 1
2. J. Stuart and D. M. Malcolm (eds.), *The Diary of Henry Francis Fyn* Pietermaritzburg, 1950.
3. N. Isaacs, *Travels and Adventures in Eastern Afric* 2 Vols., Cape Town, 1936.
4. A. F. Gardiner, *Narrati of a Journey to Zoolu Coun in South Africa*, London, 1836.
5. G. E. Cory (ed.), *The Diary of the Rev. Francis Owen*, Cape Town 1926.
6. Felix N. C. Okoye, 'Dingane: a Reappraisal', *JAH*, Vol. 2, 1969, p. 221–

response to that of the whites. This explains, although it does not justify, the massacre of Piet Retief and his companions on 6 February 1838. Moreover, it seems obvious that Dingaan was not an absolute despot; he had to consult his leading *indunas* on every important decision. In trying to buy arms to resist the whites, he was serving the interests of his people.

Mzilikazi

The same comment can be made about Mzilikazi, who maintained excellent relations with white missionaries, hunters and traders, with the obvious aim of obtaining firearms from them. Thanks to these visitors[1] and to Ndebele oral traditions collected by Malida ka Mabuya,[2] we have a good idea not only of the military stages in the formation of the Ndebele kingdom in the Transvaal, but also of the administrative methods employed by Mzilikazi.

It was at the end of 1823 that Mzilikazi, one of Chaka's leading *indunas*, rebelled against his king and left with about 300 young warriors to settle first in the area of modern Pietersburg, then from 1825 to 1832 in the outskirts of Pretoria, and finally from 1832 to 1837 in the Marico valley near the Botswana border (Zeerust area).

In 1832, the year when it was at its largest, the territory controlled by Mzilikazi extended over the western two-thirds of the Transvaal from the Limpopo to the Vaal, and its population was estimated at 100,000 people.

For twelve years by running away or by fighting, Mzikilazi managed to hold out against the Griqua and the Zulu who continually threatened him. But, powerless against the rifles of the Voortrekkers who had arrived in his territory in 1836, he decided in November 1837 to migrate yet again. North of the Limpopo, he founded the Matabele kingdom in what is now Zimbabwe (Rhodesia).

The official history abounds with descriptions of 'the aggressiveness of the black despot' and the terror he produced among the Sotho peoples, the latter presented as 'near extinction after the tyrant's visitation'.

But there is no analysis of the Ndebele political and military system, which was inspired by Chaka and his predecessor Dingiswayo. Though the military state recreated by Mzilikazi in each of his three South African phases was really perfected only in his Rhodesian phase (in Matabeleland around Bulawayo), the proof of his remarkable capacity for

1. The most important accounts we have are: R. Moffat, *Missionary Labours and Scenes in Southern Africa*, London, 1842; *The Matabele Journals of Robert Moffat 1829–1860*, edited by J. P. P. Wallis, 2 Vols., London, 1945; Andrew Smith, *The Diary of Andrew Smith 1834–1835*, edited by P. R. Kirby, 2 Vols., Cape Town, 1939–40; D. J. Kotze (ed.), *Letters of the American Missionaries 1835–1837*, Cape Town, 1950; and R. L. Cope (ed.), *Journals of the Rev. T. L. Hodgson*, Johannesburg, 1977.

2. Mziki (A. A. Campbell), *Mlimo, the Rise and Fall of the Matabele*, Pietermaritzburg, 1926.

integration lies in the fact that 10,000–20,000 Sotho ac-
companied him in his flight north at the end of 1837. This
large number suggests that the terror produced by the
Ndebele armies was not as total as the official history
indicates.

Moreover, missionaries and other visitors who recorded
their impressions were all struck by the order that reigned
in the areas controlled by Mzilikazi. It seems certain that
his policy of aggression was manifest only when he wanted
to escape from the attacks of the Zulus and the Griqua.

Without wishing to exonerate Chaka, Dingaan and
Mzilikazi completely of the charges of cruelty made against
them, we can conclude that their characters need to be seen
in a broader perspective so as to reveal their stature as
statesmen.

9 Myth IV

*That the Voortrekkers advanced
into an uninhabited land
that belonged to no one*

Versions of the myth

In *South Africa 1977*: 'After the devastation and disruption
of the Difaqane, vast sections of the interior were virtually
depopulated. It was mainly these parts that the Boer
Afrikaner pioneers populated. . . .[1] The Matabele depopulated the whole of the western Transvaal in the years 1825
to 1832.'[2]

In a Standard-6 textbook published in 1974:

Two 'Commissie Treks' sent out beforehand to gather information
about the interior (in 1834) . . . brought back very favourable
reports of fertile land and good grazing. It appeared, too, that
the land was almost uninhabited by natives. This was because
many had been massacred by the *impis* of the Zulus and the
Matabele, and the survivors were in hiding.[3]

As in the case of the preceding myths of the simultaneous
migrations of whites and blacks and the supposed habitual
nomadism of the blacks, it will be seen that school textbooks
temper to some degree the blunt statement in the Department
of Information's publication by stating that 'the survivors
were in hiding', and so implying that they would one day
reappear. This is indeed what happened—and on a very
large scale.

But the essentially temporary nature of the depopulation
of the area beyond the Orange crossed by the Voortrekkers
from 1836 onwards is never clear in the official history.

Always seeking a moral justification for the distribution
of the land, Afrikaners maintain that the Voortrekkers took
over territory that was 'uninhabited and belonged to no
one', and hence did not wrong the Africans in taking possession of it.

1. *South Africa 1977*, p. 83.
2. Ibid., p. 86.
3. *Junior Secondary History
for Standard Six*, p. 137.

Refutation of the myth

Discussion of the sources on the Difaqane

There is no denying the political and demographic upheavals brought about in much of southern Africa by the rise of the Zulu kingdom under the leadership of Chaka, the 'black Napoleon' who reigned from 1818 to 1828, when his half-brother and successor Dingaan murdered him.

After central Natal had been laid waste, many Nguni who had become subjects of the new Zulu kingdom left their country under the leadership of chiefs anxious to escape Chaka's reprisals. Some went north and founded new kingdoms in what are now Swaziland, Mozambique and even Malawi and Tanzania, 3,000 kilometres from their starting point. Others went south and settled among the Xhosa in what is now the Transkei. Still others, the most important in South African history, went west, crossed the Drakensberg passes and reached the central plateau inhabited by the Sotho.

This was the beginning, in 1822, of what is known in Sotho as the *Difaqane* and in Zulu as the *Mfecane*, i.e. 'hammering', 'crushing' or 'forced migration'.[1]

For more than ten years the Southern Sotho living in what is now the Orange Free State and on the western fringe of what is now Lesotho, and those Tswana who were settled in the southern Transvaal were subjected to continual assaults and forays which compelled them to move and to adopt similar tactics: i.e. to pillage and destroy the crops and livestock of near or more distant neighbours. The net result was a famine which decimated the population, whilst others went and took refuge in safer areas.

How many people died violent deaths in the fighting between blacks during the years of upheaval immediately preceding the Great Trek? How many died of starvation? How many fled and later returned to their birthplace to find whites settled on their land?

These are crucial questions in the context of the official history. Obviously a greatly reduced population and a small number of fugitives would, first, support the Afrikaners' traditional belief that they were within their rights in taking over uninhabited lands that belonged to no one; second, reinforce their belief that they had saved from destruction several 'small' ethnic groups which were threatened by 'large' ones and, third, persuade them that their arrival had brought order and stability to a country in the throes of disintegration (see Myth V).

1. See, for details, W. F. Ly 'The Difaqane: The Mfecan in the Southern Sotho Area 1822, 1824', *Journal of African History*, Vol. 1, 196 and J. D. Omer Cooper, *Cambridge History of Afric* Vol. 5, Ch. 9, 10, Cambridg 1976.

The most varied and fanciful answers have been given to these crucial questions; according to the author consulted, the number of South African victims, direct or indirect, of the wars set off by Chaka ranges from half a million to five million.

The weakness or absence of 'primary' sources about the Difaqane explains this diversity of views. Contemporary written accounts were written largely by missionaries. Before 1833 none of them lived in the interior of the most troubled areas of what is now the Orange Free State and southern Transvaal. The missionary Robert Moffat, who left the most detailed account we have of the Difaqane, lived at Kuruman, in former British Bechuanaland, more than 200 kilometres west of these areas from 1820 onwards.[1]

Moreover, African oral tradition was invoked only towards the end of the century, at least seventy-five years after the troubles. It varies considerably, depending on whether it is concerned with Sotho victims[2] or Zulu victors.[3] Again, African informants were often influenced by pre-existing written records, which detracts from the value of their testimony.[4]

In fact almost all historical accounts published in the twentieth century about the Difaqane are derived from G. M. Theal, whose monumental works are spread over the years 1874–1927.[5] This is true of the great 'classics' of South African history written in English, such as the works of C. E. Cory (penned between 1910 and 1932), E. A. Walker (1922–63) and W. M. MacMillan (1929–63). All repeat and sometimes amplify the devastation and carnage described by Theal. Whilst respecting the founder of historiography in South Africa, modern historians are now compelled to acknowledge that all his works are characterized by a profound contempt for the blacks, combined with a flagrant bias in favour of the white settlers.

Between the scarcity or lack of 'primary' sources concerning the events of the 1820s in what are now the Orange Free State and southern Transvaal and the obvious bias of historical accounts of this period, the relatively non-lethal character of wars between Africans at a time when they had no firearms has been completely eclipsed. The men in a group under attack often fled even before fighting. While old women and babies were often killed, young women were systematically carried off by the victorious group, and nine months later gave birth to future warriors. Without minimizing the number of people who died of starvation, it is fair to say that the number of deaths in the fighting has been greatly exaggerated by South African historians.

1. I. Shapera, *Apprenticeship at Kuruman: Being the Journals and Letters of Robert and Mary Moffat 1820–1828*, 1951.
2. D. P. Ellenberger and J. C. Macgregor, *History of the Basuto: Ancient and Modern*, 1912.
3. A. T. Bryant, *Olden Times in Zululand and Natal*, 1929.
4. S. M. Molema, *Chief Moroko*, Cape Town, 1951.
5. G. M. Theal, *Compendium of South African History and Geography*, Lovedale, 1874, and *History of South Africa*, 2 Vols., 5th ed., London, 1927.

Resettlement of Natal and the Transvaal

The speed with which the 'uninhabited' areas were reoccupied is also clear from official documents. This is very apparent in Natal, where the African population (estimated at 11,000 in 1838) was increased by 'several thousand refugees' after Dingaan's defeat at the hands of his half-brother and successor Mpande (January 1840). Indeed, it was put at 'between 80,000 and 100,000 people' in 1843, when the short-lived Republic of Natalia, proclaimed in February 1840 by Andries Pretorius, the victor of Blood River, was annexed by the British.

Two things suggest that this 1843 figure was an underestimate. First, in 1848 Andries Pretorius, who had stayed in the new British colony, abandoned the two farms he owned near Pietermaritzburg and left for the Transvaal. 'So many Zulu were living on the borders of his lands that he felt his life and property to be in danger.'[1] Second, in 1882 the African population of Natal was estimated at 375,000. The quadrupling or more in forty years that these figures imply seems difficult to accept on the basis of the natural rate of population growth.

In the Transvaal the Voortrekkers' underestimates are even more obvious if we can believe the terms of a letter written in 1884 by President Kruger to the Aborigines Protection Society. Anxious to defend himself against British accusations of ill-treatment of the natives, the President of the South African Republic of the Transvaal said that the latter 'had not been exterminated but on the contrary protected by the Boers', and gave figures to prove it: 'The natives who were placed under the protection of the Trekkers when the latter arrived in the Transvaal, some 30,000, had grown to some 700,000 by 1884.'[2] Here the figures have grown not by a factor of four, as in the case of Natal, but by a factor of twenty-three for a period of forty-eight years.

This extraordinary rate of population growth can certainly be used, as the great Afrikaner historian P. A. van Jaarsveld did, to demonstrate that the Transvaal Boers were genuinely concerned to fulfil the 'divine mission' entrusted to their fathers.

But for the foreign observer who has not been brought up in the religious mould of Afrikaner historical thinking, it is first and foremost a refutation of the doctrine that the Voortrekkers advanced into 'land that was uninhabited and belonged to no one'. It is obvious that after Mzilikazi's departure for what is now Zimbabwe in November 1837,

1. *Junior Secondary History for Standard Six*, 1974, p. 164
2. *De Express*, 16 January 1884, quoted by P. A. van Jaarsveld in *The Afrikaner's Interpretation of South African History*, Cape Town, 1964, p. 18.

the Sotho returned in great numbers to the lands from which they had been driven by the Ndebele. It is also obvious that since their own numbers were small (less than 5,000 people) and since they were widely dispersed, the white population of the Transvaal was at that time in no position to check or even estimate the size of the black population.

10 Myth V

*That only the advent of the whites saved
the blacks in the Orange Free State
and the Transvaal from total destruction*

Versions of the myth

In *South Africa 1977* we are told:

The devastation and disruption of the Difaqane affected practically every black nation in the subcontinent. . . . One can only
guess what the final toll of the Difaqane would have been, had
it not been for the arrival of the white pioneer groups. There is
much historical evidence to suggest that *the arrival of the whites
had a stabilizing effect on ethnic relations in the interior.* A period
of adjustment and consolidation followed which led to greater
clarity on the geopolitical definition of the traditional black
homelands.[1]

In a Standard-8 history book, the end of Chapter 8 about
the Great Trek (thirty-six pages out of a total of eighty-five
on the history of South Africa) states:

As we have seen, the Trekkers had to pay dearly for the land
which they inhabited in the interior. At last they destroyed the
power of the Matabeles and the Zulus. This not only meant that
territory was opened up to white settlement but also that the Wars
of Destruction, which had devastated the country and decimated
the smaller tribes, came to an end. Another result of this was that
inadvertently *the Trekkers saved the lesser tribes from annihil-
ation,* since those who had formerly terrorised the inhabitants of
the interior were now rendered powerless.[2]

The sentences we have emphasized in these two passages
give only an incomplete picture of the historical facts.

1. *South Africa 1977*, p. 83.
2. *Senior History for
Standard Eight*, 1974, p. 14(

Refutation of the myth

The Difaqane affected primarily the Southern Sotho, who lived in the eastern half of the Orange Free State.

Mzilikazi's destructive campaign was borne chiefly by the eastern group of Tswana (Western Sotho) settled in the southern Transvaal.

The north and east of the Transvaal escaped the horrors of the Difaqane. The Northern Sotho (Bapedi) were only marginally affected by Mzilikazi's conquests, and the Venda not at all. In the south-west of the Transvaal and Botswana the western group of Tswana also remained outside.

It is therefore untrue to say that 'the devastation and disruption of the Difaqane affected practically every black nation in the subcontinent'. The suggestion, so often advanced, that the blacks waited for the arrival of the whites to start a process of regeneration after the destruction of the Difaqane is also unacceptable.

The formation of new kingdoms antedated the Great Trek

An example of reconstruction antedating the Great Trek is that of the Pedi kingdom, which was attacked by Mzilikazi in 1825 but had re-established its sway in the north-east of the Transvaal by the time of the Voortrekkers' arrival.

The most famous example is that of Moshweshwe (also spelt Moshoeshoe or Moshesh).[1]

In about 1815, Moshweshwe, who, when very young, had become the head of a small clan belonging to the Kwena group of the Southern Sotho, recognized the defensive possibilities of the mountains in the north of what is now Lesotho. He systematically fortified the approaches to these heights and used them as a base for increasingly wide-ranging raids. He had already acquired a great wealth of livestock when the horrors of the Difaqane began in 1822. From then on more and more Sotho driven from their villages joined him. In 1825—eleven years before the Great Trek—Moshweshwe took refuge with 2,000 people on the top of the mountain known as Thaba Bosiu ('mountain of the night'), some twenty-five kilometres east of Maseru, the capital of Lesotho.

From this virtually impregnable stronghold he successfully withstood the successive onslaughts of the Ngwane (1827) and Mzilikazi's Ndebele (1831) and the even more dangerous ones of the Griqua and Korana (Hottentots), who had rifles and horses.

When he sent for the French Protestant missionaries,

1. P. B. Sanders, *Moshoeshoe, Chief of the Sotho*, 1974; L. M. Thompson, *Survival in Two Worlds: Moshoeshoe of Lethoso, 1786–1870*, 1975.

Moshweshwe, now known as the 'mountain king' had already managed to form a 'new nation' from the remnants of various Sotho clans fragmented and decimated by the Difaqane and many Nguni who had also been expelled from their native land.

The wars between blacks were followed by wars between blacks and whites

It must be pointed out here that as early as 1830 the new Basuto nation had re-established itself in the fertile lands of the lower Caledon valley which had been cultivated by the Southern Sotho before the Difaqane. Lesotho as created by Moshweshwe before the arrival of the whites was therefore economically viable.

But these lands, which were also claimed by the Boers after 1836, were to be the prize in wars between blacks and whites from 1848 to 1865.

In 1865 the Boers, harassed and furious at their inability to farm the richest part of the Orange Free State in peace, decided to carry out a coup by seizing all the Basuto's grain and cattle stocks. In the following year, Moshweshwe, humbled by the famine that was decimating his people and making them flee *en masse* to the hitherto uninhabited high mountains of what is now Lesotho, signed a treaty by which he ceded to the Orange Free State all the good land on the right bank of the Caledon and both banks of the lower Caledon. Consequently, British Basutoland (which became present-day Lesotho without territorial change) became a country which is hardly viable economically, as barely one-fifth of its area is arable.

This is how the rise of a black kingdom, established before the arrival of the whites, came to an end.

11 Myth VI

That the blacks' original political ideas were always inspired by whites

Versions of the myth

Unlike the myths refuted in the previous chapters, this is not a specific historical falsification, but rather a state of mind so widespread among South African whites that it is pointless to express it in terms other than the two following quotations.

In *South Africa 1977*, at the end of the section on 'Arts and Crafts' that concludes the study of 'Traditional Bantu Society':

In Africa there has been a trend to borrow ideas from foreign cultures, e.g. from India, Persia, China, the Ancient and Mediterranean world. The style developed, however, is purely African, all foreign elements have been completely absorbed. The same applies to Bantu-Africans. They rarely invent anything, but adapt all cultural attainments to their own needs and style.[1]

The Standard-6 textbook already quoted uses an account of 'Sir George Grey's native policy between 1854 and 1861' (Chapter 2) to explain to the pupils the basic inadequacies of the Bantu:

Grey was convinced that idleness, superstition and the unlimited power of the chiefs over their people lay at the root of the Bantu problem. . . . Not being accustomed to do anything else but hunt and fight, the primitive Bantu was naturally warlike. If he were taught to engage in useful and fruitful activities he would have no time or inclination for fighting.[2]

The Standard-8 textbook more discreetly suggests the black chiefs' lack of capacity for grand political designs in the chapter on 'Contacts between Bantu and Whites' (Chapter 7),

1. *South Africa 1977*, p. 93.
2. *Junior Secondary History for Standard Six*, p. 158.

by quoting the example of King Moshweshwe in 1833 welcoming the clergymen of the Paris Association of Evangelical Missions:

In 1833 the Rev. Eugène Casalis and the Rev. Thomas Arbousset set up a mission at Morija. Because of Moshweshwe's co-operative attitude progress was rapid, and by 1848 there were already eleven mission stations in the country. These French missionaries (especially Casalis) had a great influence on Moshweshwe and many of his cunning schemes originated with this missionary.[1]

Thus King Moshweshwe, one of the very few black personalities in whom the official history recognizes some positive qualities, is presented as incapable himself of having devised the 'cunning political schemes' with which he is credited.

The 'congenital inferiority of the blacks', which is merely suggested in the three previous quotations, is bluntly stated in a book by A. T. Bryant, published in 1929, from which all subsequent 'histories of the Zulus' are derived: 'The progressive ideas and activities subsequently displayed by Dingiswayo do suggest extraneous influences; for, as a pure initiative of the Bantu mind and a product of purely Bantu training, they would have been decidedly extraordinary.'[2]

The importance of this quotation lies in the fact that Chief Dingiswayo, who died in 1817, is regarded as the real inventor of the new military tactics perfected by his protégé Chaka. In particular it is he who is supposed to have replaced the traditional initiation schools with long-term military service, thus making it possible to integrate foreign elements into the 'national' army. This change was to have incalculable political consequences, and it is therefore important to ask whether it originated with blacks or whites.

Refutation

Discussion of the sources on Dingiswayo

Dingiswayo, who died in 1817, was not directly known to any white man. The trader Henry Francis Fynn, who was one of the very first whites to arrive at Port Natal (Durban) in 1824, left a 'diary' which constitutes our most complete source on Dingiswayo. Unfortunately the text of Fynn's published at Pietermaritzburg in 1950 is only a reconstruction written by the author at the end of his life to compensate for the loss of the original. This no doubt accounts for some incorrect dates, such as the one for Dingiswayo's meeting

1. *Senior Secondary History for Standard Eight*, p. 108.
2. A. T. Bryant, *Olden Time in Zululand and Natal*, 1929, p. 94.

with a certain Dr Cowan, put by Fynn at 'about 1780 or 1795'. It is now definitely established that Cowan left the Cape in 1808, and that the expedition reached the vicinity of the Limpopo river and there perished to a man.

Bryant, the author of quotation given above, was a Catholic missionary who lived in Zululand from 1883 onwards. When he set about transcribing oral traditions concerning the origins of the Zulu kingdom, three-quarters of a century had passed since Chaka had come to power. Bryant therefore tried to confirm them by referring to certain extracts from Fynn's diary published by J. Bird at Pieter-maritzburg in 1888,[1] in which he had read the account of the supposed Dingiswayo-Cowan meeting in 'about 1780 or 1795'. Here we come to the first falsification of history.

In claiming that both Dingiswayo's accession to power and also his meeting with Cowan occurred 'in 1780 or 1795', Fynn was suggesting that the latter had inspired the strategy introduced by Dingiswayo (and his successor Chaka). But moving the date of Cowan's (conjectural) travels in Zululand to 1808 weakened the argument considerably. This did not bother Bryant, who simply shifted Dingiswayo's accession to power to 1808.[2]

Similarly second falsification of history Bryant resorted to truncated genealogies to show that the Zulus arrived in South Africa in the middle of the seventeenth century.

The theme of the white inspiration of Dingiswayo's political and military thought was taken up again in 1875 in a revised form by Theophilus Shepstone. According to Shepstone, Dingiswayo in his youth entered the service of a settler at Cape Colony.

Both versions, equally fanciful, have been repeated in several 'histories of the Zulus' published since, and have never been refuted in the official history.

Moshweshwe and the French missionaries

We saw in the previous chapter that the founding of the kingdom of Lesotho antedated by several years the arrival of the French protestant missionaries in 1833. While the latter were valuable advisers, they did not inspire the political thinking of the 'Mountain King'.

1. J. Bird (ed.), *The Annals of Natal, 1495–1845*, Pietersmaritzburg, 1888.
2. S. Marks, 'The Traditions of the Natal Nguni: A Second Look at the Work of A. T. Bryant', in L. M. Thompson (ed.), *African Societies in Southern Africa*, 1969.

12 Myth VII

*That the Afrikaners were victims
of British imperialism
and were not colonialists*

If land distribution in South Africa is the result of a colonial conquest similar to any other, it follows that it is no longer 'historically' justifiable now, when all the former colonial powers have yielded land ownership and political rights to the Africans.

To counter this criticism, Afrikaners claim that their position as a 'white tribe' established on South African soil for over three centuries is unprecedented in Africa. Here they are right. They also claim that nineteenth-century British imperialism was solely responsible for the 'colonial situation' in South Africa, and that having been victims of this imperialism themselves, they are absolved of the sin of colonialism. Here they are wrong, as this chapter will show.

Versions of the myth

In *South Africa 1977*: 'Present-day South Africa is as much multinational as it is multiethnic. The political and social boundaries which delineate this population structure are mainly the result of British colonial history in Southern Africa.'[1]

The following picture of British imperialism is painted on page 206:

In the course of the nineteenth century those units which today comprise the territorial contents of South Africa were two Boer republics, the two colonies of the Cape and Natal and several independent Black nations, such as the Zulu and Xhosa nations. *It was due to the British colonial policy at the time that these independent nations were, through a series of annexations, forced*

1. *South Africa 1977*, p. 210

together under a single political authority (the British Crown). This artificial unity brought into political juxtaposition disparate and incompatible ethnic and racial groups, particularly the white Boer-Afrikaners on the one hand and nine principal Black (Bantu) peoples on the other.[1]

The italicized passages of the text assert that the London Government was solely responsible for the colonial situation in South Africa.

But the Afrikaners go still further, and say that they cannot be taxed with colonialism or imperialism since they were themselves victims. This is what J. B. Vorster, Prime Minister at the time, said (in Afrikaans) in his famous Nigel speech on 5 November 1974: 'We are not imperialists and we are not colonialists. Small as we were and poor as we were, we were the first African country to take a stand, first against Dutch colonialism and later against English imperialism.[2]

Refutation

The argument does not apply to the seven homelands in the Transvaal and the Orange Free State

Like other demonstrations of Afrikaner 'rights', the falsification lies not in what is said but in what is omitted.

The Zulu and Xhosa 'nations', which are the only ones referred to in the quotation above, have been given three homelands. The Transkei and the Ciskei are in Cape Province, and KwaZulu in Natal Province.

There is no question that these homelands, which taken together represent over half of all South African blacks, are the result of the policy of annexation adopted by London between 1866 (the annexation of Kaffraria or Kaffirland, part of which became the Ciskei) and 1897 (the annexation of Zululand). So are the three protectorates of Basutoland (Lesotho), Bechuanaland (Botswana) and Swaziland, which became independent in 1966 and 1968.

But it is no accident that *South Africa 1977* avoids using the term 'nation' when it speaks of the 'diversity of the principal peoples and their incompatibility with the Afrikaners'. For though the seven other 'principal black peoples' are classified as 'nations' under the apartheid system, they were certainly colonized just like the Xhosa and Zulu. The difference is that they were colonized by the Afrikaners in the two Boer Republics. In other words, during the nineteenth

1. *South Africa 177*, p. 206.
2. Nigel speech,
5 November 1974 (original in Afrikaans).

century, the Afrikaners (Boers) were simultaneously the
colonial subjects of the British and the colonizers of the
black inhabitants of the Transvaal and Orange Free State.
In the latter role they used exactly the same methods of
conquest or purchase as the other colonial powers in
Africa.

The 'colonial' nature of the relationship
between whites and blacks
in the nineteenth-century Boer republics

As elsewhere, the 'right of conquest' acquired through the
superiority of European arms was extended to a much
larger area than that in which a defeated African chief had
actually exercised his authority. Thus after Mzilikazi had
fled northward after the battle of Kapain in November 1837,
'Potgieter considered that the whole area over which Mzilikazi
had ruled now belonged to the Trekkers by right of conquest.
Thus the territory between the Vet and the Limpopo Rivers
was declared Voortrekker territory'.[1] Now it is clear that
the area actually under Mzilikazi's control was limited at
that time to the western Transvaal.

As elsewhere, treaties were 'signed' by chiefs putting
their mark at the foot of documents totally inconsistent
with the African conception of land ownership. Thus the
treaty drawn up by Piet Retief and signed by Dingaan on
4 February 1838 (two days before he had Piet Retief and his
seventy comrades killed) granted the Voortrekkers 'perpetual
ownership of all the land between the Tugela and Umzimvubu
rivers'. Now it was unthinkable for an African king, to
give up part of the land belonging to his people permanently,
except by war, since he was only its manager.

As elsewhere, land was 'purchased' for absurdly low
prices. For instance, the northern half of the Orange Free
State went to Andries Potgieter early in 1836 for twenty-
nine head of cattle[2] and a promise to protect Chief Makwana
against the Matabele. Since the area between the rivers
Vet and Vaal represented some 60,000 square kilometres,
Potgieter got 2,000 square kilometres per head of livestock.
The terms of this exchange might strike South African
secondary-school pupils as unfair, which is no doubt why
the author of the Standard-8 textbook already quoted refrains
from giving the details: 'Potgieter was given the territory
between the Vet and the Vaal Rivers by Makwana, the
Bataung Chief. In return for this Potgieter gave him some
cattle and promised to protect his tribe from the Matabele.'[3]

1. *Junior Secondary Histor*
for Standard Six, p. 161,
2. Freda Troup, *South*
Africa, an Historical
Introduction, 1975, p. 113.
3. *Senior Secondary Histor*
for Standard Eight, p. 121.

As elsewhere, the Afrikaner 'colonizers' encountered strong and sustained 'local resistance', some of which seriously endangered them. The history books mention only a few examples:

Potgieter and a number of his people left Potchefstroom in 1845 . . . for the Eastern Transvaal where they laid out a new town called Ohrigstad (north of Lydenburg) near the Portuguese border. Bantu tribes in the area were very hostile and until Potgieter punished them life in the town was very unsafe. . . .[1]

In 1867 in the Zoutpansberg various Bantu tribes . . . began to attack the Boers in Schoemansdal. A commando led by Commandant General Paul Kruger which hastened to their aid was forced to retreat and most of the white inhabitants of Schoemansdal fled for safety.[2]

In 1871 Burgers [the newly elected President] found very difficult circumstances existing in the Transvaal. Money was scarce, Bantu tribes threatened the country. . . . In the Lydenburg district Sekukunya, chief of the Bapedi tribe, was becoming a threat to the Republic. He did not regard himself and his people as subject to the Boers and refused to pay taxes. In 1876 a commando sent against him was unable to drive him out of his mountain fortress. The whole campaign was a miserable failure.[3]

Like the other colonial powers, but much sooner after the conquest, the Afrikaners regarded their new black subjects as 'cheap labour'. As early as 1841, in the first short-lived Boer Republic of Natalia, the Volksraad (People's Assembly) decided to 'drive all blacks not working for the whites beyond the Umtamvuna River' (now the border between Natal and the Transkei).

The Transvaal republics adopted a similar system. Blacks who were not in the service of the white farmers were sent to 'locations' (precursors of the 'native reserves' which were to become the Bantustans and then the homelands), systematically sited on the worst land and administered by native chiefs who were themselves liable to taxation payable in livestock or labour.

The 'land policy' of the Afrikaners in the nineteenth century can only be described as colonialist. Indeed, it was even more colonialist than that of the other colonial powers. There is no equivalent elsewhere of the way in which white land was acquired during the Great Trek. The Voortrekkers and their children re-established on the 'uninhabited' lands of the Orange Free State and Transvaal the old Dutch system which the British administration had made them relinquish. After prospecting the area in search of the best land, the

1. *Junior Secondary History for Standard Six*, p. 163.
2. Ibid., p. 172.
3. Ibid., p. 183.

farmer fixed the centre of his property and demarcated its boundaries by riding for half an hour in the four directions of the compass. If one or more potential native landowners appeared, they were either allowed to work for the white farmer or driven into a 'location'.

In short, neither the method of colonial settlement (conquest or land purchase) nor that used to create a cheap labour force to work differentiates Boer 'colonialism' in the republics from British 'imperialism' in the two colonies of the Cape and Natal.

13   Myth VIII

*That the major goal
of the 1913 and 1936 Land Acts was
to protect black lands from the whites*

The first official demarcation of the 'native reserves', which became 'Bantustans' in the 1960s and are today known as 'black homelands', was approved by the Parliament of the Union of South Africa in 1913.

Under the 1913 Native Land Act the 4 million blacks registered in the 1911 census were allotted permanent and inalienable ownership of 8.9 million hectares distributed throughout all four provinces.

The figures for the separate provinces give a clear idea of the situation created for the blacks. In the Transvaal, for example, over a million blacks had absolute ownership of 425,000 hectares, while it was illegal for them to buy any of the 26 million hectares set aside for 300,000 whites. In Natal 100,000 whites had 6.5 million hectares, as compared with 2 million hectares allocated to approximately one million blacks. In the Orange Free State thousands of squatters were evicted from one day to the next in the middle of the southern winter.

Versions of the myth

In view of these figures it is difficult to claim that 'the 1913 Native Land Act was passed in a spirit of fairness and justice with the object of protecting the tribal lands of the blacks'. Yet this is what the official history claims. We propose to quote first *Histoire de l'Afrique du Sud*, published in French in 1972 by the Pretoria Department of Information. Virtually the same text appears in *South Africa 1977* (Chapter 3, 'History', p. 39–62):

The Native Land Act was passed in 1913. . . . The major significance of this Act lay in the fact that it introduced the principle of a territorial division of the country between the Bantu and the whites. Under the terms of this Act, some 8.9 million hectares of land, situated in the four provinces and chiefly in the east of the Cape Province, were demarcated, registered and allocated to the Bantu on a permanent and inalienable basis. This Act prevents whites and non-whites from buying each other's land, and protects their respective rights. In this way, it decisively safeguards the tribal lands of the Bantu against being 'eroded' by the economically stronger Europeans. The 1913 Native Land Act represents a sincere wish to lay down the broad lines of an equitable national policy.[1]

In Chapter 12, 'Multinational Development', *South Africa 1977* briefly analyses the 1913 Native Land Act (incorrectly referred to as the Bantu Land Act) and ends by stating: 'At the same time the black territories were protected against occupation by the economically stronger and more developed whites.'[2] South Africa 1977 goes on to stress the improvement in the blacks' land situation brought about by the 1936 Act: 'In addition, the Bantu Trust and Land Act of 1936 provided for another 6.3 million hectares of land to the black homelands. This increased the designated land area of the black peoples by almost 70 per cent, from 92,000 km² to 154,000. . . .'[3]

Refutation

The 1936 Act

The preceding quotation contains two glaring errors. The native reserves occupied 8.9 million hectares at the bottom of page 204, but ten lines later, at the top of page 205, they cover 92,000 km². Moreover, in 1936 the blacks were referred to as natives, and the name of the Act is the Native (not Bantu) Trust and Land Act. But this is not the major issue. As with other 'myths', the falsification lies not in what is said but in what is omitted. The first omission occurs in de Kock's statement that 'The Native Trust and Land Act gave effect to the provisions in the Native Land Act of 1913 for the purchase of land for the Bantu populations'.[4] Actually the area of the reserves, which was equivalent to 7.2 per cent of the total area of the Union, seemed so inadequate that the Act contained provisions for enlarging it. From 1914 to 1918 the Beaumont Commission, set up for this purpose, carried out a thorough investigation and recommended a 70-per-cent increase. But twenty-three years elapsed before

1. W. J. de Kock, *Histoire l'Afrique du Sud*, p. 25.
2. *South Africa 1977*, p. 20
3. Ibid., p. 204, 205.
4. de Kock, op. cit., p. 37.

Parliament decided to approve the implementation of these recommendations.

Another fact not stated is that the prescribed land purchases were carried out with extraordinary slowness, and that by the end of 1976 1.2 million hectares, a quarter of the area set aside forty years before, still remained to be purchased.

Nor is it stated that in the sixty-five years that have elapsed since 1913 the population of the reserves (which became Bantustans and then homelands) has quadrupled while their area has increased only one and a half times, and that this situation has been denounced by all the political leaders of the homelands as incompatible with real independence.

The second omission is the close connection between the Native Trust and Land Act and the Representation of Natives Act of 1936. The latter deprived the few Africans who were on the electoral roll in the Cape Province of the right to vote on the same lists as the whites (in the other three provinces the blacks were not entitled to vote), while the former deprived them of the right to buy land outside the reserves, and so reduced them to the condition of all other South African blacks.

These two Acts, passed in the same year, thus represent an important step towards apartheid; they codified the political and territorial separation of whites and blacks.

The third omission is that the 1936 Act recommended stopping individual land purchases (allowed under the 1913 Act) and provided for the establishment of a South African Native Trust on the pattern of the 1864 Natal Act which would buy land on behalf of African communities and supervise its use. In so doing it strengthened the authority of the chiefs but prevented the formation of a prosperous black peasant class, which was one of the causes of the rapid decline of agriculture in the homelands.

The 1913 Act

While recognizing that the 1913 Act protected the rights of whites and blacks, W. J. de Kock stresses the fact that it 'safeguards the tribal lands of the Bantu against being eroded by the economically stronger Europeans'. In fact, the purpose of this Act was just the opposite. It was primarily to protect white lands by prohibiting blacks from buying any land outside the native reserves and limiting the growth of black squatting.

Since the last quarter of the nineteenth century the dearth of arable land for whites and blacks alike had led to the settlement of large numbers of landless peasants or squatters on the vast estates owned by the whites. They paid their rent either by working for nothing for a predetermined period (labour tenants) or by giving the landowner a predetermined proportion (generally half) of the crops or the increase in the herds. This latter system of sharecropping was increasingly criticized by white landowners, who saw in it an infringement of the master/servant relationship established in the early days of white colonization.[1]

In the Orange Free State the 1913 Act was interpreted as reinforcing previous legislation against black squatting. When it was published many white farmers immediately evicted large numbers of black squatters, forcing them to sell their herds at poor prices and leave their shelters in mid-winter.[2]

In the western Transvaal white farmers complained mainly about blacks buying land on the many white estates abandoned at the end of the Boer War (1899–1902), either because the buildings had been burnt down by the British or because the owners had not returned. The *South African Native Affairs Commission* set up by Lord Milner in 1903 reported that 'the natives are beginning to buy land around Johannesburg in order themselves to produce food for the new markets on the Rand'. After 1905 the whites became uneasy about these co-ownership purchases by associations of blacks pooling their savings, because they were becoming increasingly frequent and, in particular, because the death of one of the co-owners inevitably led to complications unknown in the case of individual ownership.

It was to allay their fears that the main clause of the 1913 Act was adopted, prohibiting blacks from buying any land outside the African reserves (which, it should be noted, occupied 7 per cent of the national territory).

1. 'The half-share system is a pernicious system, because it takes away from your neighbour natives who ought to be servants.' Report of the Beaumont Commission, 1916, quoted by H. R. Davenport, *South Africa, A Modern History*, p. 335.
2. Sol T. Plaatje, *Native Life in South Africa before and since the European War and the Boer Rebellion*, London, 1916.

14 Myths IX and X

That the homelands correspond to the areas historically occupied by each black 'nation' and that their fragmentation was the result of tribal wars and succession disputes

The two myths considered in this chapter could just as well have served as an introduction to Part Three about falsifications in the official history of the South African blacks: the statement that the homelands represent the traditional tribal territories of each of the black nations is an essential element of the 'historical justification' of apartheid.

Versions of the myth

The clearest version of this myth is to be found in a Standard-7 history book: 'The Government's argument is that the Bantu reserves correspond roughly to the areas occupied by the Bantu when the Whites and Blacks first encountered each other in Southern Africa.'[1]

South Africa 1977 no longer refers to 'Bantu reserves' but to 'black homelands' or 'traditional tribal territories':

By the end of the nineteenth century the forbears of all those blacks at present settled within the country had been brought under the political authority and guardianship of the whites. The nuclei of the various ethnic groups retained their traditional tribal areas. Today these are known as the black homelands.[2]

On the next page it is stated that 'after the Difaqane the remnants of the various black peoples concentrated in those areas which are to this day their traditional homelands'. And, dealing more specifically with the Tswana: 'After the new white communities had put a stop to tribal wars, the Tswana moved gradually back to their old homelands, seeking protection under the trusteeship of the whites as they had done before the OFS.'[3]

1. *Junior Secondary History for Standard Seven*, 1974, p. 133.
2. *South Africa 1977*, p. 82.
3. Ibid., p. 83.

In short, we are asked to believe that the Tswana and Southern Sotho, dispersed by the Difaqane, deliberately came back to absolutely uninhabitable areas such as the Kalahari desert, which covers four-fifths of what is now Botswana, or the high mountains that cover three-quarters of what is now Lesotho. Or else, looking only at the homelands of South African blacks, we are asked to believe that the Tswana voluntarily settled in the dry, barren areas that make up present-day Bophuthatswana, only 6.6 per cent of whose land is arable.

It is hardly likely. But the zealots of apartheid take absurdity even further when they give reasons for the fragmentation of the homelands:

The fragmentary appearance of the Black homelands is chiefly the result of tribal wars and succession disputes; the Blacks settled in comparatively small areas because their migrations were tribal movements rather than major population shifts involving full-fledged nations. This explains the rash of small tribal lands that came into being as the southward migrations dissipated themselves in the subcontinent.[1]

Refutation

The fragmentation of the homelands

In the land of apartheid there is no more awkward subject of discussion than the fragmentation of the homelands. Even sympathizers of the regime express surprise at a degree of fragmentation, which seems inconsistent with the usual idea of independence. They find it difficult to accept, for instance, that in order to visit the whole of his 'State', which has been 'independent' since 6 December 1977, the President of Bophuthatswana must cross the borders of the white Republic twelve times. For Bophuthatswaba was divided into seven fragments in 1978, three in the north of Cape Province, three in the north-western Transvaal and a seventh in the Orange Free State, over 600 kilometres from the nearest other fragment.

KwaZulu—which refuses independence—was to have consisted of ten pieces according to the 'final' regrouping plans published in March 1975. In fact the purchases of 'white land' needed for the regrouping are far from complete, and the situation is not very different from that of 1974, when KwaZulu was divided into 44 pieces and 144 'black spots'. These black spots are the estates bought by the blacks

1. *South Africa 1977*, p. 206.

before 1913 when they were allowed to do so. To the traveller on the roads of Natal they are immediately obvious because of the neglected look of the crops and the poverty of the environment, which contrast strongly with the vast estates (planted with sugar-cane in the coastal area) belonging to the white settlers.

Although the whites ascribe these differences to the laziness and incompetence of the blacks, it is obvious that the prime causes are first the poor quality of the land that has been abandoned to the blacks and, second, the lack of administrative support (loans, preferential prices or irrigation) for native agriculture.

In the light of these elementary facts the historical reasons for the fragmentation presented on page 206 of *South Africa 1977* are simply untenable. This is particularly true of Natal, since, as the official history tells us, the country south of the Tugela was virtually uninhabited when the Voortrekkers in 1840 proclaimed the Republic of Natalia. It is precisely in the third of KwaZulu south of the Tugela that fragmentation is most pronounced. Nearly all the 144 'black spots' listed in 1975 are in this area, as are approximately 30 'pieces' out of 44.

In the case of KwaZulu it is really impossible to blame 'tribal wars and succession disputes' for a fragmentation due solely to the land hunger of the white settlers (mostly British in southern Natal).

As to the homelands of the three Sotho groups, we have seen that two-thirds of the Transvaal and three-quarters of the Orange Free State were peopled by Sotho at the end of the eighteenth century.

As in other parts of the world, the distribution of peoples who live by cattle-breeding and agriculture has developed in relation to local water resources. In areas with good water resources such as the south-western Transvaal, aerial photography has shown the extraordinary density of native settlement, although this did not prevent the whites from establishing themselves there as exclusive owners of the land. It should be noted that this region, the cradle of Sotho settlement between the eleventh and the sixteenth centuries, now lies entirely within the 'white area'.

The division of Bophuthatswana and Lebowa (Northern Sotho) into seven pieces each (nineteen and fifteen pieces respectively before 1975) postdates the arrival of the whites, who took the best land for themselves and drove the blacks into the barren areas.

The location and size of the homelands

The third Sotho homeland is Qwaqwa, the homeland of the Southern Sotho.

If all the Southern Sotho (or Shweshwe), estimated in 1976 at 1.6 million people, came and settled there, population density would be over 3,200 people per square kilometre. It is a tiny mountain region of 457 square kilometres situated in the Orange Free State north of Lesotho without any agricultural or mineral resources or any major road, rail or air links. In 1970 Qwaqwa was inhabited by only 24,000 Southern Sotho, or 2 per cent of its 'citizens'. Although in 1976 the official figures rose to 144,000, or 9 per cent, it is obvious that the vast majority of Southern Sotho will always be comdemned to live outside their 'national home'.

So wide a disparity between the *de facto* and the *de jure* population is hard to reconcile with the theory that 'the homelands are the traditional tribal areas occupied by the different ethnic groups when they encountered the whites for the first time'. On that basis the real homeland of 1.6 million South African blacks belonging to the Shweshwe linguistic group is not tiny Qwaqwa (situated on South African territory) but Lesotho, an independent country since 1966 populated by 1.2 million Southern Sotho. There would be no difficulty in merging the two homelands.

While such a merger may seem logical to whites it is unacceptable to the blacks, since more than one-fifth of the Sotho of Lesotho are compelled to look for work in South Africa because of the extreme poverty of their country—this poverty being a direct result of the wars waged between King Moshweshwe and the Boers of the Orange Free State between 1848 and 1865. As we have seen, the 1866 Treaty of Aliwal North gave the Boers more than half the arable land in the Caledon valley and forced the Basuto either to take refuge in the hitherto uninhabited mountains of what is now Lesotho or to enter the service of the whites.

Hence Lesotho and Qwaqwa only partly fit the official historical definition of the homelands as the 'traditional tribal areas at the time of the whites' arrival'.

The same may be said of the Ciskei. The 5,300 square kilometres of this second Xhosa homeland (the first being the Transkei, a territory of 41,000 square kilometres proclaimed 'independent' on 26 October 1976) represent less than half the territory between the Kei River (the border between the Transkei and the Ciskei) and the Great Fish River (the southern border of the Ciskei). We have seen that when the border of the Dutch Cape Colony was pushed back to Great Fish River in 1778, the Xhosa not only occupied all the land between the Kei and Great Fish Rivers but also overflowed well south of Great Fish River into the rich grazing lands of the Zuurveld (now the Grahamstown area).

In 1779 the commando leader Adriaan van Jaarsveld drove several thousand oxen stolen from the Xhosa south of Great Fish River. This event started the first 'Kaffir War'.[1]

There was a second Kaffir War in 1789, a third between 1799 and 1803 and a fourth in 1811–12. They always followed the same pattern. The Xhosa crossed the border, were accused of stealing livestock and were pursued by the settlers into the territory north of Great Fish River that was recognized as belonging to them.

After the fifth Kaffir War (1818–19), the British governor changed tactics and had the 'neutral zone' between the Fish and Keiskama rivers (in the south of what is now the Transkei) evacuated; then he changed his mind and allowed the Xhosa to occupy it again. The same cycle began again, with Boer commandos penetrating into Xhosa territory for livestock.

The sixth Kaffir War began in 1834, the year of the emancipation of slaves. It was followed by the annexation of the Xhosa territory between the Keiskama and Kei rivers, which was designated as Queen Adelaide Province. Another change in British policy in 1836 gave Queen Adelaide Province its independence. This considerably increased the insecurity of the Boer farmers on the border and was one of the causes of the Great Trek.

In 1847 a seventh Kaffir War broke out and at its end the former Queen Adelaide Province was renamed British Kaffraria and placed under military control. An eighth Kaffir War in 1850–53 did not change the political situation, but increased the Xhosa's feeling of frustration at having their livestock and above all their lands progressively whittled away over a period of fifty years.

This feeling of being driven by the whites to the point of losing their nationhood is certainly at the root of what has been called 'the national suicide of the Xhosa'.[2] In March 1856 a 16-year old Xhosa girl called Nongqase had a vision and announced that all the whites would leave the country the following August if the blacks slaughtered all their livestock and destroyed all their reserves of grain. The Xhosa obeyed her in large numbers, and a terrible famine ensued which brought about the death of between 20,000

1. C. Saunders, 'The 100 Years' War', in D. S. Chanaiwa (ed.), *Profiles of Self-determination*, 1977.
2. R. Ralston, 'Xhosa Cattle Killing, 1856–57', op. cit.

and 60,000 people and over 200,000 head of cattle. The few survivors left for Cape Colony. The British Government took advantage of this situation from 1858 onwards to move new settlers into British Kaffraria (the hinterland of the port of East London, founded in 1848), including several thousand recruited from the 'German Legion' of the Crimean War. By 1860 there were 6,000 of them, and the Xhosa who came back to their country after the tragedy of 1856 found their land occupied. British Kaffraria was finally annexed to Cape Colony in 1866.

The case of the Transkei is different. According to the supporters of apartheid its size (41,000 square kilometres, i.e. the largest of all the homelands) and the fact that it is divided into only three pieces are proof of the good faith of the whites and, at the same time, a guarantee of economic viability. It is true that by comparison with the other home-lands the Transkei seems to be favoured in these respects, but this is not due to the whites' good will. All the literature published at the time of the Transkei's 'independence' carefully avoids saying that Tembuland (the southern half of the Transkei) was ceded to the British Cape Colony by its Chief Gangelizwe in 1875 and that, because of the resist-ance of its inhabitants, Pondoland (the northern half of the Transkei) was annexed only in 1894, fifty-six years after the Sotho who occupied the western Transvaal had as a matter of course been regarded as 'subjects' of the Voor-trekkers after Mzilikazi's defeat.

Hence, if the Transkei more or less corresponds to the area historically occupied by the Xhosa, Tembu and Pondo after Chaka's wars, it is because they managed to maintain their independence much later than the Sotho of the Transvaal and the Orange Free State. Moreover, the Xhosa of the Ciskei shielded the Transkei against the advance of the white settlers during the eight Kaffir Wars between 1779 and 1853.

Part Four:
Conclusions

15 The rejection
of historical truth

'Justifying' the land distribution or systematically denigrating
and disparaging the South African blacks are the two aims,
pursued for the most part simultaneously, of the ten historical
myths presented and refuted in the preceding pages.

But still more serious than the falsifications of specific
points is the pervasive rejection of two essential aspects of
South African history, namely history as seen by blacks
and history as made by blacks in the modern period.

Rejection of the history
of the blacks as seen by blacks

In an article published in 1972 Steve Biko, the 'father of Black
Consciousness', who died in prison on 12 September 1977,
wrote:

The history of the black man in this country is most disappointing
to read. It is presented merely as a long succession of defeats.
The Xhosa were thieves who went to war for stolen property;
the Boers never provoked the Xhosas but merely went on
'punitive expeditions' to teach the thieves a lesson. . . . Great
nation-builders like Shaka are cruel tyrants who frequently
attacked smaller tribes for no reason but for some sadistic
purpose. Not only is there no objectivity in the history taught us
but there is frequently an appalling misrepresentation of facts
that sicken even the uninformed student. If we as blacks want to
aid each other in our coming into consciousness we have to rewrite
our history and produce in it the heroes that formed the core of
our resistance to the white invaders. . . . We would be too naive to
expect our conquerors to write unbiased history about us but
we have to destroy the myth that our history starts in 1652, the
year Van Riebeeck landed at the Cape.[1]

. Steve Biko, 'Black
Consciousness and the Quest
for a True Humanity', in
Basil Moore (ed.),
Black Theology, 1973.

In point of fact the task of reconstructing the history of South African blacks had already been attempted, but under conditions such that Steve Biko and the 1976 generation of black students were not generally told about it.

The first three historical works signed by African authors appeared in 1952, the year in which Afrikaners enthusiastically celebrated the third centenary of Van Riebeeck's landing. The timing was of course no coincidence, for one of the main myths rightly denounced by Steve Biko is that the history of all South Africans began in 1652, whereas in fact this date applies only to the Afrikaners.

In a long analysis of these three books, the historian F. A. van Jaarsveld[1] quotes several particularly significant passages from Nosipho Majeke and Mnguni. Majeke wrote: 'The story, if truly told, is one of continuous plunder of land and cattle by the European invaders, of the devastation and decimation of people, followed by their economic enslavement.'[2] Mnguni, after giving a very similar definition of history as seen by the oppressed, set out his long-term objective:

The purpose of this history is to expose the process of conquest, dispossession, enslavement, segregation and disfranchisement of the oppressed non-Europeans of South Africa in order that the oppressed as a whole will understand better how to transform the *status quo* into a society worth living for and worth living in.[3]

It should be noted here that the impact of the last sentence went far beyond the limited circle of intellectuals for whom it was presumably intended. The year 1952, like 1960 (Sharpeville) and 1976 (Soweto), was one of the 'great years' of the history of the African resistance movement, as may be seen from the following calendar of events.

In June, two months after the tricentenary celebrations, the African National Congress (ANC) launched the Defiance Campaign against 'unjust laws', notably the Pass Laws and the Group Areas Act passed in 1950. In six months 8,500 Africans and Indians (who had been seriously affected by the application of the Group Areas Act, which deprived Indian tradesmen of their African customers) were arrested for deliberate violation of the discriminatory legislation. They included J. S. Moroka and Dadoo, chairmen of the ANC and the SAIC (South African Indian Congress) respectively, who were arrested in August under the Suppression of Communism Act.

In October, at the time of the proclamation of the state of emergency against the Mau-Mau revolt in Kenya (where

1. Van Jaarsveld, op. cit., p. 151–4.
2. Nosipho Majeke, *The Role of the Missionaries in Conquest*, Johannesburg, 1952.
3. Mnguni, *A History of South Africa*, Cape Town, 1952.

many settlers were of South African origin), riots broke out in several towns and were harshly put down. Officially there were forty African deaths and several hundred casualties.

Finally in December, Albert Luthuli, who had been elected in place of Moroka as Chairman of the ANC (which then had an active membership of over 100,000) was 'deposed' from his Zulu chieftaincy by Pretoria and immediately 'banned' for two years.

It seems clear that the Defiance Campaign and the 1952 riots resulted both in a strengthening of the repressive legislation and in an upsurge of political awareness among new classes of African society. The latter was to lead to the adoption of the Freedom Charter (1955) and the foundation of the Pan Africanist Congress (1959).

The third historical work published by a black South African in 1952 undoubtedly aroused the greatest interest at the time. It was a pamphlet called *Three Centuries of Wrong*, which was published in the middle of the tricentenary celebrations. The author, Dr S. M. Molema (known for his ethnological studies on the Xhosa), drew a parallel between the Boers' long historical struggle against British domination and the 'fight for freedom' waged by blacks today. He also pointed out that 'Afrikaners should not forget that the subjected and oppressed of today might become the rulers and legislators of tomorrow'.[1]

Since 1952 repression and censorship have been continually intensified, culminating in the arrest of 3,500 persons between January and June 1963 and the sentencing of the main ANC leaders to life imprisonment in June 1964. They included Govan Mbeki, whose remarkable historical and sociological study of the black peasants' revolt was to be published in London in the same year.[2]

Under these conditions it is hardly surprising that black intellectuals were reticent about such a dangerous field as history. They thought, rightly, that they could serve the cause of resistance better through the theatre, and particularly through poetry,[3] which would be more effective methods of mobilizing the general public. For black South Africans, therefore, 1952 was the first and last year for publishing historical works.

Rejection of history made by blacks

After the brutal 1963–64 repression of the resistance movements sprung from the ANC and the PAC (both declared illegal in 1960), the deep apathy of the urbanized black

1. Van Jaarsveld, op. cit., p. 152.
2. Govan Mbeki, *South Africa: the Peasants' Revolt*, 1964.
3. J. Alvarez-Pereyre, *Les Guetteurs de l'Aube. Poésie et Apartheid*, 1979.

masses reinforced the feeling of the whites that 'the Blacks are socio-politically inassimilable'. By a typically Afrikaner method of reasoning, this assumption is presented both as the cause and the effect of the absolute refusal to give urbanized blacks political rights, even if they have been city-dwellers for three generations.

This is what Chapter 13 of *South Africa 1977*, on 'The black Outside the Homelands', seeks to demonstrate: 'The fact that a black worker in a white city displays all the external and material signs of the western life-style does not necessarily mean that he has fully absorbed the Western value system.[1] And a little further on:

The non-homelands blacks cherish their distinctive ethnic and historical identities. By and large, these communities are ethnic extensions of the black homelands and their political status is bound up with the national development of these homelands. This policy flows logically from the white Republic's insistence that the non-homeland Blacks are regarded by the white nation as socio-politically inassimilable.[2]

In practice the government has developed a policy of compulsory retribalization in the townships, especially in the oldest and most densely populated ones such as those at Soweto. This policy is applied in residential areas, and is particularly evident in education.

Thus the twenty-six townships that make up Soweto (the abbreviation of South Western Townships), south-west of Johannesburg, are regarded as mono-ethnic. The reservation of one or more of these townships for Zulu, Xhosa, Southern Sotho, Northern Sotho, etc., results in the creation of ethnic sub-ghettoes within the black ghetto.

In the long term, the educational system introduced in 1953 by the Bantu Education Act reinforces this ethnic segregation, which has been imposed on the inhabitants of Soweto against their will. All primary education up to and including Standard 5 (i.e. 83 per cent of pupils in white areas in 1974) is given exclusively in the pupils' mother tongue. By contrast, all the governements of the homelands decided in 1974 to introduce English and English alone as the language of instruction from Standard 3 upwards. (Only secondary-school children were affected by the attempt to introduce compulsory Afrikaans as the second language of instruction in 1976.)

The tribalization of education for black children in white areas is only one aspect of the deplorably low level of this education, which the ratio of public expenditure per child

1. *South Africa 1977*, p. 22
2. Ibid., p. 230.

suffices to demonstrate. For 1975/76 the average cost per pupil was R644 for whites (for whom education is free), R190 for Indians, R140 for coloureds and R42 (or fifteen times less than for whites) for blacks, who have to pay for education.

The pretence of purely consultative municipal councils for the townships represented by the Urban Bantu Councils, established in 1961 and abolished in 1977, was based on tribal foundations. In Soweto, for instance, seventeen members were appointed by representatives of the homeland governments and forty-one elected by the residents on the basis of ethnic lists.

In trying to retribalize the urbanized blacks, Pretoria is swimming against the tide of history and elementary logic.

Throughout the world the massive movement of rural people to an urban environment has led to familiar sociological and psychological upheavals. The government admits this as regards the Afrikaners (only 10 per cent of whom were urbanized at the beginning of the century). In *South Africa 1977* we read: 'The Afrikaner's culture (formed in a rural context) has been significantly affected by the modern urban way of life.'[1]

At the same time, however, Pretoria utterly refuses to recognize that similar changes can occur in the blacks' culture and mentality, although some of them were urbanized earlier than the Afrikaners. In 1911 out of the 658,000 whites living in towns (52 per cent of the white population) there were barely more than 50,000 Afrikaners, ten times less than the number of blacks (508,000 or 13 per cent of the black population) officially registered as urbanized.

With a similar lack of logic *South Africa 1977* reports with satisfaction 'the existence of a black middle class consisting of 60,000 families in 1976' (p. 228) and recognizes the 'weakening of tribal and ethnic affiliations' in that class (p. 229). But the government has systematically located in the homelands 68 per cent of the secondary schools and all the three 'university colleges' for the children of this black middle class.

The decision to bar blacks from the two so-called 'open' white universities (Cape Town and the University of the Witwatersrand, to which they had been admitted) dates from 1959, the year in which the Extension of University Education Act set up the three ethnic university colleges: the University of the North (at Turfloop, in Lebowa) reserved for the Sotho, Tswana, Tsonga and Shangaan; the University of Zululand, reserved for the Zulu and Swazi; and the

1. *South Africa 1977*, p. 81.

University of Fort Hare (in the Ciskei) for the Xhosa.
In 1977 the three 'residential university colleges for blacks'
together had just over 5,000 students, while 6,000 African
students were enrolled in correspondence courses at the
University of South Africa in Pretoria. In the same year
15,500 certificates and degrees were awarded in eleven white
universities with 111,000 students, and 1,760 to black students
out of an enrolment of 11,500.

The Pretoria Government thought that by setting up
three 'university colleges for blacks' it had perfected the
edifice so carefully erected against any advancement for
blacks within white society. It was making a great mistake,
for these university ghettoes were actually to be the birthplace
of the Black Consciousness movement.

In 1969 Steve Biko (1946–77), a medical student at the
University of Durban, founded together with other 'non-
white' students the South African Students' Organization
(SASO), as organization separate from NUSAS, the National
Union of South African (English-speaking) students, for all
the oppressed of South African society who rejected the 'negative' collective designation of 'non-whites' and demanded
the 'positive' term 'blacks'.

In 1971, Steve Biko played a part in founding the Black
People's Convention (BPC). Then in 1972, together with
Bennie Khoapa and Bokwe Mafuna, he was appointed to
take charge of the Black Community Programme (BCP),
aimed at increasing the awareness of the black community.

At the same time dissent was developing in the black
universities. On 29 April 1972 Abraham Tiro, a former mine-
worker turned student at the University of the North,
selected to speak on behalf of the 'Student Council' at the
official graduation ceremony, strongly attacked 'Bantu Education', and called for one educational system for all four
racial groups in South Africa. He vehemently stressed the
ruthless control exercised by whites at every level of black
student life, and ended with the following words: 'Let the
Lord be praised, for the day shall come when all shall be
free to breathe the air of freedom which is theirs to breathe,
and when that day shall have come, no man, no matter how
many tanks he has, will reverse the course of events.'[1]

Three days after these 'scandalous' words, Abraham Tiro
was expelled from the university. For the next two months
the three black universities, the coloured university college
at Belville (near Cape Town) and the Indian university
college at Durban were emptied of their students. At the
beginning of 1973 five-year banning orders were served on

1. Quoted by Denis
Herbstein in *White Man, W
Want to Talk to You*, 1978,
p. 73.

eight black student leaders, including Steve Biko and Barney Pityana, past chairmen of SASO, and Mondisane, the current chairman. Abraham Tiro, who had managed to escape to Botswana, was killed in February 1974 by a parcel bomb sent from Geneva by BOSS (Bureau of State Security).

We have thought it essential to dwell somewhat on the 'Abraham Tiro affair', because of its consequences. The main ones include the foundation (in 1973) of the South African Students Movement (SASM), which was to play a decisive part in the 1976 riots, and the rapid spread of the Black Consciousness ideology through black theatre and poetry. An article written by Steve Biko in 1972 defined this ideology:

/Black Consciousness is an attitude of mind and a way of life. The philosophy of Black Consciousness expresses group pride and the determination of the black to rise and attain the envisaged self. . . .) At the heart of this kind of thinking is the realization by blacks that the most potent weapon in the hands of the oppressor is the mind of the oppressed. . . . We have to evolve our own schemes, forms and strategies to suit the need and situation, always keeping in mind our fundamental beliefs and values.[1]

In short, Steve Biko called upon blacks to cast aside their inferiority complexes and exalt their own system of values.

This is a genuine 'cultural revolution', the outcome of a radical change of mentality—just the kind of change the Pretoria government denies has taken place. It is just as dynamic a factor in the contemporary history of South Africa as white initiatives.

The second dynamic factor in history made by blacks is economic. It also appeared in 1973. The great Durban strikes between 9 January and the end of March involved over 61,000 African workers (nearly all Zulu), and made the blacks aware of the power they wield as workers.

Following those strikes, not only did the employers grant the wage increase they had continuously refused previously but, even more important, the government passed new labour legislation[2] establishing a system of black worker representation in 'works committees' and 'liaison committees'; this did not, however, bring about any change in the situation of African trade unions, which remained 'authorized' but 'non-recognized': that is, not empowered to put forward the claims of their members to the employers or to the State.

The new Act also legalized the right to strike for blacks, but only in certain circumstances so restrictively defined that all subsequent movements have been unofficial strikes. The strike ban affects all black public service employees and, in

1. Quoted by A. M. Goguel and P. Buis in *Chrétiens d'Afrique du Sud face à l'Apartheid*, 1978, p. 135–6.
2. The Bantu Labour Regulation Amendment Act, approved in May 1973, modifying the 1953 Native Labour (Settlement of Disputes) Act.

the private sector, domestic staff, farm labourers, transport workers and those employed in gold-mining and coal-mining. Offenders are liable to maximum penalties of 1,000 rand and three years' imprisonment (200 rand and one year's imprisonment for whites, coloureds and Asians).

Six years later, this time at the instance of the employers, a new stage began with the decision of the Botha Government to grant to all black South African workers, including 'citizens' of the three 'independent' homelands, as of 1 October 1979, the right to join a union. Regarded by many as a means of keeping a closer check on the activities of existing black trade unions, this authorization considerably strengthens the negotiating power of those who register.

In point of fact, while meeting the wishes long expressed by employers bent on competitiveness in foreign markets, Pretoria is seeking to form a black middle class whose role it will be, as the Prime Minister puts it, 'to fight alongside the whites against Marxist forces of destruction'. But the interaction between economic and political policies which today benefits the whites will no doubt, tomorrow or the day after, work in favour of the blacks.

16   Towards the future

Although the practice of extrapolation in history is dangerous and should be strongly discouraged, it seems necessary to extrapolate in concluding this study on apartheid and history. Since the discovery of diamonds (1870) and the gold of the Witwatersrand (1886), the economy of South Africa has relied on black labour.

The Second World War and the tremendous industrial expansion that followed led to a massive upsurge in black urbanization, which is now increasing almost exponentially. The race of black urbanization rose from 22 per cent (1.7 million) in 1946 to 33 per cent (5.3 million) in 1970. According to estimates published by the official *Africa Institute Bulletin*, it should reach 56 per cent (10 million) in 1978[1] and 75 per cent (27 million) in the year 2000 for a total population (blacks + whites + coloureds + Indians) of 48 million.[2]

According to the same sources, the black working population will rise from 7 million in 1975 to 13.6 million in the year 2000, or 78 per cent of the total working population (18.7 million). Of these 13.6 million black workers there will be at least 3 million skilled workers, whose training needs to be planned as quickly as possible.

The integration of blacks in the white economy is continually on the increase. Whereas previously they were merely cheap labour, they represent today a purchasing power indispensable to the health of the white economy, and tomorrow a source of skilled manpower equally essential to the whites.

Whilst recognizing the necessity for the economic integration of the blacks, apartheid (or multinational development) is utterly opposed to their sociopolitical integration.

1. *Africa Institute Bulletin*, No. 6, 1978, p. 206.
2. Ibid., No. 4–5, 1978, p. 157, 158.

The Pretoria Government takes this suicidal contradiction to its limits by increasing repression. On 19 October 1977, five weeks after Steve Biko's death in prison, it banned eighteen organizations associated with Black Consciousness and had more than fifty people arrested or banned. On the same day the *World*, with a daily circulation of 160,000, and its supplement the *Weekend World* were forced to stop publication.

In thus opposing the black resistance 'preventively', the government believes that it can stem the course of history. But this is self-deception.

Since Soweto the wind of history has changed. The whites are no longer the absolute masters of South African history. Even if the government's power still seems assured for many years, the blacks have now lifted up their heads. They have shed the feeling of inferiority which was their weakness. International pressure can only accelerate their inevitable emancipation.

Bibliography

The place is not given for English titles published in London or French titles published in Paris.

General histories of South Africa

Official works quoted in the text

Junior Secondary History for Standard Six. Cape Town, 1974.
Junior Secondary History for Standard Seven. Cape Town, 1974.
Senior Secondary History for Standard Eight. Cape Town, 1975.
History and Geography for Standard Eight. Cape Town, 1975.
Standard Encyclopaedia of South Africa, Vol. 10, 1973; Vol. 12, 1976.
South Africa 1977. Pretoria, 1978.
DE KOCK, W. J. *Histoire de l'Afrique du Sud.* Pretoria, 1972.

Selected recent titles

The Cambridge History of Africa, Vol. 4, 1600–1790, p. 439–58, 1975; Vol. 5, 1790–1870, p. 353–93, 1976; Vol. 3, 1050–1600, p. 597–620, 1977.
CHRISTOPHER, A. *Southern Africa: An Historical Geography.* 1976.
CORNEVIN, R. *Histoire de l'Afrique*, Vol. I, 2nd ed., p. 102–35, 1966; Vol. III, p. 17–73, 1975.
DAVENPORT, T. R. H. *South Africa: A Modern History.* 1977.
HOUGHTON, D. H. *The South African Economy*, 4th ed. 1976.
JOOS, L. C. D. *Histoire de l'Afrique du Sud.* 1965.
LACOUR-GAYET, R. *Histoire de l'Afrique du Sud.* 1970.
LESOURD, J. A. *La République d'Afrique du Sud.* 1968.
MAGUBANE, B. *The Politics of History in South Africa.* United Nations Notes and Documents, Centre Against Apartheid, July 1978.
The Oxford History of South Africa, Vol. I (to 1870), Oxford, 1969; Vol. 2 (1870–1966), 1971.
PARKER, G.; PFUKANI, P. *History of Southern Africa.* 1975.
TROUP, F. *South-Africa: An Historical Introduction.* 1975.

Contemporary South Africa

This section includes only recent works on domestic policy, i.e. apartheid. It should be noted that many of the titles in English are prohibited in South Africa.

ADLER, T. (ed.). *Perspectives on South Africa*. African Studies Institute, University of Witwatersrand, 1977.

AFRICA BUREAU. *The Great White Hoax, South Africa's International Propaganda Machine*. 1977.

ALVAREZ-PÉREYRE, J. *Les Guetteurs de l'Aube, Poésie et Apartheid*. University of Grenoble, 1979.

BENSON, M. *Struggle for a Birthright*. 1966.

BERNETEL, P. *Les Enfants de Soweto: L'Afrique du Sud en Question*. 1977.

BIKO, S. *I Write What I Like*. 1978.

Black Review. Produced by the Black Communities Programme, 5 Vol. 1972–76.

BOESAK, A. *Farewell to Innocence: a Socio-ethical Study of Black Theology and Black Power*. Braamfontein, 1977.

BUNDY, C. *The Rise and Fall of the South African Peasantry*. 1979.

BUTLER, J. et al. *The Black Homelands of South Africa*. Berkeley, 1978.

CALLINICOS, A.; ROGERS, J. *Southern Africa after Soweto*. 1977.

CORNEVIN, M. *L'Afrique du Sud en Sursis*. 1977.

DAVIS, D. *African Workers and Apartheid*. 1978.

DESMOND, C. *Christians or Capitalists? (Christianity and Politics in South Africa)*. 1978.

——. *The Discarded People*. 1972.

FRIEDMAN, J. R. *The Republic of South Africa and Apartheid: Basic Facts*. United Nations Notes and Documents, April 1977.

GOGUEL, A. M.; BUIS, P. *Chrétiens d'Afrique du Sud Face à l'Apartheid*. 1978.

HERBSTEIN, D. *White Man, We Want to Talk to You*. 1978.

HIRSON, B. *Year of Fire, Year of Ash*. 1979.

JOHNSON, R. W. *How Long Will South Africa Survive?* 1977.

JOHNSTONE, F. A. *Class Race and Gold: A Study of Class Relations and Racial Discrimination in South Africa*. 1976.

KANE-BERMAN, J. *Soweto. Black Revolt, White Reaction*. Braamfontein, 1978.

LACHARTRE, B. *Luttes Ouvrières et Libération en Afrique du Sud*. 1977.

LEFORT, P. *L'Afrique du Sud. Histoire d'une Crise*. 1977.

LIMP, W. *Anatomie de l'Apartheid*. 1972.

MANGANY, M. C. *Being Black in the World*. Braamfontein, 1973.

MARE, G. (ed.). *The Durban Strikes, 1973*, 1976.

MOORE, B. (ed.). *Black Theology, The South African Voice*. 1973.

NGUBANE, J. K. *An African Explains Apartheid*. 1963, repr. 1978.

NKONDO, G. M. *Turfloop Testimony, the Dilemma of a Black University in South Africa*. Braamfontein, 1976.

ROBERTSON, E.; WHITTEN, P. (eds.). *Race and Politics in South Africa*. 1978.

ROGERS, B. *Divide and Rule: South Africa's Bantustans*. 1976.

RUBIN, L. *Apartheid in Practice*. United Nations Information Service, 1976.

SIKAKANE, J. *Window on Soweto*. IDAF, 1977.

Société Africaine de Culture (Présence Africaine). *L'Afrique du Sud Aujourd'hui*. 1978.

South African Institute of Race Relations. *A Survey of Race Relations in South Africa*. 1976, 1977.

Thoahlane, T. *Black Renaissance*. Braamfontein, 1976.

Thomas, D. (ed.). *Liberation*. Johannesburg, 1976.

Troup, F. *Forbidden Pastures, Education under Apartheid*. 1976.

Unesco. *Apartheid: Its Effects on Education, Science, Culture and Information*, 2nd ed. 1972.

——. *Racism and Apartheid in Southern Africa*. 1975.

Vaillant, F. (ed. and trans.). *Poètes Noirs de l'Afrique du Sud*. 1975.

Van der Pol, C. *et al*. *The Urgent Need for Fundamental Change in South Africa*. 1977.

Wilson, F. *Migrant Labour in South Africa*. Braamfontein, 1972.

Wolfson, J. G. E. (ed.). *Turmoil at Turfloop*. SAIRR, 1976.

Woods, D. *Steve Biko: Life and Death*. 1978.

The historical-religious amalgam

Agar-Hamilton, J. A. I. *The Native Policy of the Voortrekkers*. Cape Town, 1928.

——. *The Road to the North*, 1939.

Arnold, G. *The Last Bunker: A Report on White South Africa Today*. 1976.

Bunting, B. *The Rise of the South African Reich*. 1964.

De Klerk, W. A. *The Puritans in Africa: A Story of Afrikanerdom*. 1975, 2nd ed. 1976.

Du Toit, S. *Holy Scriptures and Race Relations*. Potchefstroom, 1960.

Elphick, B. *Kraaland Castle: Khoikkoi and the Founding of White South Africa*. New Haven, Conn., 1977.

Jaarsveld, F. A. van. *The Afrikaner's Interpretation of South African History*. Cape Town, 1964.

——. *The Awakening of Afrikaner Nationalism*. Cape Town, 1961.

Macmillan, W. M. *Bantu, Boer and Briton*, rev. ed. Oxford, 1963.

Moodie, T. D. *The Rise of Afrikanerdom: Power, Apartheid and the Afrikaner Civil Religion*. Berkeley, Calif., 1975.

Randall, P. (ed.). *Apartheid and the Church*. Johannesburg, 1970.

Setfontein, J. H. P. *Brotherhood of Power, An Exposé of the Secret Afrikaner Broederbond*. 1979.

Simons, H. J.; Simons, R. E. *Class and Colour in South Africa, 1850–1950*. 1969.

Sundermayer, T. (ed.). *Church and Nationalism in South Africa*. Johannesburg, 1975.

Thion, S. *Le Pouvoir Pâle*. 1969.

Vaatcher, H. *White Laager, The Rise of Afrikaner Nationalism*. New York, 1965.

Welsh, D. *The Roots of Segregation: Native Policy in Colonial Natal, 1845–1910*. Cape Town, 1972.

History of South African blacks to the end of the eighteenth century (myths I and II)

Articles

DAVIES, O. Excavations at the Walled Early Iron Age Site in Moor Park near Eastcourt, Natal. *Annals of Natal Museum,* 1974, p. 289–323.

DERRICOURT, R. M.; EVERS, T. M. Robertsdrift, an Iron Age Site and Settlement near Standerton, South-eastern Transvaal. *African Studies,* 1973, p. 32.

EHRET, C. *et al.* Outlining Southern African History: a Reconsideration, A.D. 100–1500. *Ufuhamu,* Vol. I, 1972.

EVERS, T. M. Recent Iron Age Research in the Eastern Transvaal. *South African Archaeolgical Bulletin,* 1975, p. 71–83.

EVERS, T. M.; VAN DEN BERG, R. P. Ancient Mining in Southern Africa. *Journal of the South African Institute of Mining and Metallurgy,* 1974, p. 217–26.

FAGAN, B. The Grefswald Sequence: Bambandyanalo and Mapungubwe. *Journal of African History,* 1964, p. 337–63.

INSKEEP, R. R.; MAGGS, T. Unique Art Objects in the Iron Age of the Transvaal. *South African Archaeological Bulletin,* 1975, p. 114–38.

KLAPWYK, M. An Early Iron Age Site near Tzaneen, N.E. Transvaal. *South African Journal of Science,* 1973, p. 324.

MAGGS, T. M. O'C. Ntshetane, An Early Iron Age Site in the Tugela Basin, *Annals of the Natal Museum,* Vol. 3, 1976.

——. Iron Age patterns and Sotho History on the Southern Highveld of South Africa. *World Archaeology,* Vol. 7, 1976.

——. Some Recent Radiocarbon Dates from Eastern and Southern Africa. *Journal of African History,* Vol. 2, 1977.

——. South Africa before Van Riebeeck; Some Results of Archaelogical Research. *Reality,* Vol. I, 1978.

MASON, R. J. Background to the Transvaal Iron Age, New Discoveries at Olifantspoort and Broederstroom. *Journal of the South African Institute of Mining and Metallurgy,* 1974, p. 211–16.

——. Transvaal and Natal Iron Age Settlement Revealed by Aerial Photography and Excavation. *African Studies,* 1968, p. 27.

MASON, R. J. *et al.* The Early Iron Age Settlements of Southern Africa. *South African Journal of Science,* 1973.

PRINSLOO, H. P. Early Iron Age Site at Klein Afrika near Vylliespoort, Soutpansberg Mountains, South Africa. *South African Journal of Science,* 1974, p. 70.

SMITH, A. The Peoples of Southern Mozambique: An Historical Survey. *Journal of African History,* Vol. 4, 1973.

VAN DER MERWE, J. J.; SCULLY, R. T. K. The Phalaborwa Story: Archaelogical and Ethnographic Investigation of a South African Iron Age Group. *World Archaeology,* Vol. 3, 1971.

WILSON, M. The Early History of the Transkei and Ciskei, *African Studies,* Vol. 4, 1959.

Books

BIRMINGHAM, D.; MARKS, S. Southern Africa. In *Cambridge History of Africa,* Vol. 3, Ch. 8. Cambridge, 1977.

DERRICOURT, R. M. *Prehistoric Man in the Ciskei and Transkei.* Cape Town, 1977.

FOUCHÉ, L. *Mapungubwe, Ancient Bantu Civilisation on the Limpopo.* Cambridge, 1937.

GALLOWAY, A. *The Skeletal Remains of Bambandyanalo.* Johannesburg, 1959.

GARDNER, G. M. *Mapungubwe*, Vol. 2. Pretoria, 1963.

GRAY, R.; BIRMINGHAM, D. (eds.). *Precolonial African Trade.* 1970. (In particular: A. Smith, Delagoa Bay and the Trade of South Eastern Africa, p. 265–89.)

MARKS, S. In *Cambridge History of Africa*, Vol. 4, Ch. 6. Cambridge, 1975.

OLIVER, R.; FAGAN, B. M. *Africa in the Iron Age.* Cambridge, 1975.

SAUNDERS, C.; DERRICOURT, R. (eds.). *Beyond Cape Frontier, Studies in the History of the Transkei and Ciskei.* 1974.

THOMPSON, L. (ed.). *African Societies in Southern Africa.* 1969. (See particularly M. Legassik, The Sotho Tswana Peoples before 1800, p. 86–125.)

WILSON, M. *Oxford History of South Africa*, Vol. 1, 1969, p. 75–186.

History of South African blacks in the nineteenth century (myths III to VII)

Books: contemporary accounts

ALBERTI, L. *Description Physique et Historique des Cafres.* Amsterdam, 1811.

ARBOUSSET, T. *Voyage d'Exploration au Nord-Est de la Colonie du Cap de Bonne-Espérance.* 1842. English trans., Cape Town, 1846 and 1968.

BIRD, J. (ed.). *The Annals of Natal*, 1495 to 1845. Pietermaritzburg, 1888. Extracts from the diary of H. P. Fynn, p. 60–71, 73–93, 95–124.

BURCHELL, W. J. *Travels in the Interior of South Africa.* 1822. New ed., 2 Vols., 1953.

CAMPBELL, J. *Travels in South Africa, 1813–1815.* 1820, 2 Vols., 1822.

CAPE, R. L. (ed.). *Journals of the Rev. T. L. Hodgson.* Johannesburg, 1977.

CASALIS, E. *Les Bassoutos.* 1839, new ed., 1930. English trans., London, 1861; Cape Town, 1965.

DELEGORGUE, A. *Voyage dans l'Afrique Australe de 1838 à 1844.* 2 Vols., 1847.

FYNN, H. F. *The Diary of Henry Francis Fynn.* Ed. by I. Stuart and D. M. Malcolm. Pietermaritzburg, 1950.

GARDINER, A. F. *Narrative of a Journey to the Zoolu Country.* 1836.

ISAACS, N. *Travels and Adventures in Eastern Africa.* 1836. Ed. by L. Herman, 2 Vols., Cape Town, 1935–36.

KOTZÉ, D. J. (ed.). *Letters of the American Missionaries, 1835–1838.* Cape Town, 1950.

LICHTENSTEIN, H. *Travels in Southern Africa in the Years 1803–1804.* 1805. 2 Vols., Cape Town, 1928, 1930.

MOFFAT, R. *Matabele Journals.* Ed. by J. P. R. Wallis, 1945.

——. *Missionaries' labours and scenes in southern Africa.* 1842.

MOFFAT, R.; MOFFAT, M. *Apprenticeship at Kuruman.* Ed. by I. Shapera, 1951.

OWEN, F. *The Diary of the Rev. Francis Owen.* Ed. by G. E. Cory, Cape Town, 1926.

PRINGLE, T. *Narrative of a Residence in South Afrika.* 1835.
SMITH, A. *The Diary of Andrew Smith, 1834–1836.* Ed. by P. R. Kirby,
2 Vols., Cape Town, 1939–40.

Selected books

BRYANT, A. T. *A History of the Zulu and Neighbouring Tribes.* Cape
Town, 1965.
——. *Olden Times in Zululand and Natal.* 1929. Cape Town, 1965.
——. *The Zulu People.* Pietermaritzburg, 1949.
CHANAIWA, D. S. (ed.). *Profiles of Self-determination: African Responses
to European Colonialism in Southern Africa, 1652–present. 1977.* (See
in particular: R. Ralston, Xhosa Cattle Killing, 1856–57; C. Saunders,
The 100 Years' War.)
COPE, A. T. *Izibongo, Zulu Praise Poems.* Oxford, 1968.
ELLENBERGER, D. P.; MACGREGOR, J. C. *History of the Basuto Ancient
and Modern.* 1912.
HAMMOND TOKE (ed.). *The Bantu-speaking Peoples of Southern Africa.*
1974.
MOFOLO, T. *Chaka the Zulu.* 1931. (Translated from Sesotho.)
MOLEMA, S. M. *Chief Moroko.* Cape Town, 1951.
MORRIS, D. R. *The Washing of the Spears: a History of the Rise of
the Zulu Nation under Shaka and its Fall in the Zulu War of 1879.*
New York, 1965.
MZIKI (A. A. Campbell). *Mlimo, the Rise and Fall of the Matabele.*
Pietermaritzburg, 1926.
OMER-COOPER, J. D. In *Cambridge History of Africa,* Vol. 5, Ch. 9, 10.
Cambridge, 1976.
——. *The Zulu Aftermath.* 1966.
RASMUSSEN, R. K. *Migrant Kingdom: Mzilikazi's Ndebele in South
Africa.* London/Cape Town, 1978.
SANDERS, P. B. *Moshoeshoe, Chief of the Sotho.* 1974.
THOMPSON, L. M. (ed.). *African Societies in Southern Africa.* 1969.
(See in particular: W. F. Lye, The Distribution of the Sotho Peoples
after the Difaqane; S. Marks, The Traditions of the Natal Nguni:
A Second Look at the Work of A. T. Bryant; A. Smith, The Trade
of Delegoa Bay as a Factor in Nguni Politics, 1750–1835, p. 171–89.)
——. *Survival in Two Worlds, Moshoeshoe of Lethoso, 1786–1870.*
Oxford, 1975.
THOMPSON, L. M.; WILSON, M. (eds.). *The Oxford History of South
Africa,* Vol. 1 (to 1870). Oxford, 1969.

Articles

LYE, W. F. The Difaqane: the Mfecane in the Southern Sotho Area,
1822–1824. *Journal of African History,* Vol. 1, 1967.
——. The Ndebele Kingdom South of the Limpopo River. *Journal of
African History,* Vol. 1, 1969.
MARKS, S. Shaka Zulu. In *Les Africains,* Vol. II, p. 283–307. 1977.
OKOYE, F. N. C. Dingane: a Reappraisal. *Journal of African History,*
Vol. 2, 1969.
SANDERS, P. B. Sekonyela and Moshweshwe. *Journal of African History,*
Vol. 3, 1969.
SMITH, K. W. The Fall of the Bapedi of the North-Eastern Transvaal.
Journal of African History, Vol. 2, 1969.

[A.24] PUB.79/X.3/